THE CONFEDERATE WAR

The Confederate War

GARY W. GALLAGHER

Harvard University Press
Cambridge, Massachusetts
London, England

First Harvard University Press paperback edition, 1999

Library of Congress Cataloging-in-Publication Data

Gallagher, Gary W.
The Confederate War / Gary W. Gallagher.
p.   cm.
Includes bibliographical references and index.
ISBN 0-674-16055-X (cloth)
ISBN 0-674-16056-8 (pbk.)
1. Confederate States of America—Historiography.
2. United States—History—Civil War, 1861–1865—Historiography.
3. Confederate States of America—Social conditions.   I. Title.
E487.G26   1997
973.7′13—dc21   97-2495

Title page illustration: Charleston harbor battery during the Civil War.

For Barnes F. Lathrop,
a master graduate teacher who pointed out
the delights and responsibilities of studying the past

ACKNOWLEDGMENTS

....

The invitation to give the 1995–96 Littlefield endowed lectures at the University of Texas at Austin came as a wonderful surprise. It afforded an opportunity to focus my thinking about several major themes relating to the Confederacy—especially the ways in which those themes have been addressed by historians over the past several decades. The lectures also allowed me to return for a brief time to the Department of History at Texas, where I spent my graduate career. I believe in the adage that you can't go home again, but the visit to Austin and the University could not have been more pleasant.

I was fortunate to have Barnes F. Lathrop as my major professor at Texas. His astonishing grasp of the materials relating to Confederate history, unflinching refusal to tolerate sloppy thinking or writing, and willingness to lavish attention on the work of his students set an impressive standard of graduate teaching. Many decades of support from the Littlefield Fund have given Texas a breathtaking array of manuscript and printed materials on the mid-nineteenth-century South, and I have fond memories of roaming the stacks of the library (then housed in the tower of Old Main) to track down obscure items Lathrop mentioned in our many long conversations about southern and Confederate historiography. This book's dedication attests to my continuing debt to a treasured mentor and friend.

I wish to thank all the members of the Littlefield lectureship committee for their help and support. Lewis L. Gould extended the invitation to give the lectures and looked after many details. Shearer Davis Bowman, Norman D. Brown, and Robert A. Divine joined Lew Gould in overseeing the lectures, and Bonnie Montgomery, who has helped keep the Department of History at Texas running smoothly for many years, handled logistics with her usual unerring competence.

William A. Blair, Richard M. McMurry, and T. Michael Parrish read drafts of this book and suggested many improvements. Their attention to the manuscript follows years of informal discussion of Confederate history from which I have benefited immensely. The value of such friends cannot be overestimated.

Eileen Anne Gallagher displayed her habitual tolerance for my testiness as the deadline for completion of the project drew near. She insists that years of work on Jubal A. Early have taken their toll on my own personality. If that notion helps her cope with a sometimes difficult spouse, I suppose I should nod approvingly in Old Jube's direction.

Contents

....

THE CONFEDERATE WAR

INTRODUCTION

THE CHALLENGE OF THE CONFEDERATE EXPERIENCE

Scholarship on the Confederacy over the past several decades has yielded a paradoxical result. Historians have exploited a variety of sources and approaches to illuminate many facets of the Confederate experience, but the overall effect of much of this work has been to distort the broader picture. Moving beyond traditional emphases on military events, politics, and prominent leaders, many recent scholars, concentrating on the analytical categories of race, class, and gender, have highlighted social tensions and fissures to create a portrait of Confederate society crumbling from within by the mid-point of the Civil War. All too aware that the Confederacy failed in its bid for independence, many historians have worked backward from Appomattox to explain that failure. They argue that the Confederates lacked sufficient will to win the war, never developed a strong collective national identity, and pursued a flawed military strategy that wasted precious manpower. Often lost is the fact that a majority of white southerners steadfastly supported their nascent republic, and that Confederate arms more than once almost persuaded the North that the price of subduing the rebellious states would be too high.[1]

....

Although class tension, unhappiness with intrusive government policies, desertion, and war weariness all form part of the Confederate mosaic, they must be set against the larger picture of thousands of soldiers persevering against mounting odds, civilians enduring great human and material hardship in pursuit of independence, and southern white society maintaining remarkable resiliency until the last stage of the war. Part of the problem stems from a failure to place the Confederate people's wartime behavior within a larger historical framework. If historians choose to label Confederates as lacking in will and national sentiment, they should do so with an eye toward how white Americans have responded to other major traumas.

Academic historians have led the way in positing an absence of strong national will in the Confederacy, but popular writers have joined in the chorus. In this vein, Robert Penn Warren observed in 1980 that Jefferson Davis, Robert E. Lee, and many of their fellow Confederates failed to embrace secession with any enthusiasm. A horrific war soon exposed the absence of both solid ideological underpinning for their republic and widespread common purpose among its people. By the later stages of the conflict, noted Warren, "Merely some notion of Southern identity remained, however hazy or fuddled; it was not until after Appomattox that the conception of Southern identity truly bloomed—a mystical conception, vague but bright, floating high beyond criticism of brutal circumstances."[2]

More often than their academic counterparts, popular writers have veered toward a romantic conclusion that the Confederacy fought gallantly against hopeless odds. In the pictorial history of the Civil War that accompanied Ken Burns's film documentary, for example, Shelby Foote pronounced the Confederate bid for independence doomed from the start. "I think that the North fought that war with one hand behind its back," observed Foote. If the Confederacy ever had come close to winning on the battlefield, "the North simply would have brought that other arm out from behind its back. I don't think the South ever had a chance to win that war." Foote also claimed that white southerners knew their cause was hopeless well before the end of the conflict. Heavy casualties, shortages of goods behind the lines, and loss of faith in European recognition promoted a "realization that defeat was foreordained." As so many historians over the years have done, Foote turned to South Carolina diarist Mary Chesnut for a summary quotation to clinch his points: "It's like a Greek tragedy, where you know what the outcome is bound to be," wrote Chesnut. "We're living a Greek tragedy."[3]

Wartime testimony contradicts both Foote's assessment and the prevalent scholarly image of a Confederate populace only weakly committed to winning independence. Letters, diaries, and newspapers reveal a widespread expectation of Confederate success and tenacious popular will rooted in a sense of national community and closely attuned to military events. In March 1864, a point in the war when many modern scholars describe a Confederacy enveloped in despair and defeatism, Lucy W. Otey penned a letter that evinced common sentiments. Alluding to contributions of clothing for soldiers in Lee's army, Otey observed that "they are raised through the energetic and persevering efforts of *Southern Women* who can never faint or tire, in animating and sustaining the brave Soldiery of this Confederacy, while struggling for our Independence!" So long as the men remained in the field, stated Otey, "there are loving hearts and busy hands *at home*—praying and toiling, for their preservation and success!" Eight months later a young woman in Milledgeville, Georgia, lamented the fall of her city to Federal troops but expressed undiminished loyalty to the Confederacy: "The yankee flag waved from the Capitol—Our degredation was bitter, but we knew it could not be long, and we never desponded, our trust was still strong. No, we went through the house singing, 'We live and die with Davis.' How can they hope to subjugate the South. The people are firmer than ever before."[4]

A pair of letters from the summer of 1864 illuminate the optimism and willingness to fight on for months or years characteristic of many Confederates. "I used to think I could see some end to the War," wrote a sailor in the Confederate navy from Savannah, Georgia, adding, "I don't see any chance for it to close at all." Still, this man remained optimistic and committed for the long term: "I know the Yankees cannot, nor never will, whip us. I do think it depends entirely on the election of the next President of Yankeedom whether we have peace for the next five years to come." From the trenches near Petersburg, Virginia, Luther Rice Mills of the 26th Virginia Infantry anticipated a resounding Confederate success. "I am expecting Lee to take the offensive," wrote Mills to his father on June 6. "Perhaps he will allow

Grant to butt his head a few more times & destroy more of his men and then pitch into him. I think Lee will attempt to capture Grant's whole army. His chance for it seems to be quite good."[5] These letters, together with countless others voicing comparable sentiments, contrasted sharply with the profound disenchantment with the war expressed by many northern soldiers and civilians during the same period. Had the North lost the war, historians doubtless would have used its people's literary record to prove a lack of will that helped explain Confederate success.

Far from being a loosely knit collection of individuals whose primary allegiance lay with their states, a substantial portion of the Confederate people identified strongly with their southern republic. Wartime writings frequently employed language that revealed a sense of national community. A North Carolina soldier touched on often-repeated themes in a letter of March 1864. "I feel that the cause is a just one and am willing to spend the balance of my days in the army rather than give up to a relentless foe that shows no mercy and will give none," stated Rufus A. Barrier. "Let us stand firm by our country's flag and we are bound to succeed." Barrier went on to castigate the "little souled mercenaries who are croaking so loudly and are willing to sell their country for filthy lucre and let their names be handed down to posterity branded with the curse of being traitors to their country." A Georgian in Lee's army, writing to his wife on his twenty-fourth birthday in the spring of 1864, echoed Barrier's feelings of national loyalty. "When we consider the great duty we owe our country in the struggle for independence, I cannot be but content with my fate, although it be, indeed, a cruel one," affirmed Daniel Pope. "I am determined to do anything and everything I can for my country," he continued. "If it should be my misfortune to fall in the glorious struggle, I hope that I shall go believing that I have contributed my mite and that you and my little boy will be entitled to the great boon of freedom."[6]

As the war progressed, Confederate citizens increasingly relied on their armies rather than on their central government to boost morale, and Robert E. Lee and his Army of Northern Virginia eventually became the most important national institution. This phenomenon has received far too little attention—perhaps because of a tendency in the scholarly literature to slight the vital ways in which military events influenced the home front. Comments by the deputy executive director of the American Historical Association in 1990 typify the inclination among academic historians to play down the military side of the conflict. Addressing a congressional committee on the topic of battlefield preservation, James B. Gardner claimed to speak for the broad historical community in remarking that "historians today have redefined the study of the Civil War, shifting attention from military action to the diverse experiences of individual groups, the impact of emancipation," and the ways in which the war exacerbated old social divisions and created new ones. In calling for a shift away from "narrow, antiquated views" of history represented by undue attention to Civil War battles and generals, Gardner manifested a stunning innocence of the ways in which military events helped shape all the dimensions of American life he considered important. (In fairness, it must be acknowledged that military historians interested primarily in battles and campaigns similarly have slighted the impact of the home front on the armies.)[7]

Whatever subsequent generations of historians thought, people living through the war understood the centrality of military events to national morale and, by extension, to the outcome of the war. In June 1863, a Georgia newspaper printed a letter that clearly tied the spirit behind the lines to the actions of Confederate armies: "In breathless but hopeful anxiety, the public are awaiting the result of Lee's movements at the North and [Joseph E.] Johnston's at the South," commented the author. "Upon their success hang momentous interests—no less to our mind than an early peace or the continuance of the war for an indefinite period." Edward A. O'Neal, Jr., an Alabamian whose father commanded a brigade in Lee's army, wrote in October 1863 that offensive victories would bolster civilian morale buffeted by the battles of the preceding summer. O'Neal believed "our existence as a nation depends on it. Forebearance is no longer a virtue with us. The people are gloomy, and weary of this 'never ending—still beginning' strife, and victory alone will revive their drooping spirits." The war's most famous instance of linking home front and battlefield came from north of the Potomac River when, in March 1865, Abraham Lincoln spoke in his second inaugural address of "The progress of our arms, upon which all else chiefly depends." Well might Lincoln remind northerners of this linkage, for he almost certainly would have been defeated for re-election had William Tecumseh Sherman and Philip H. Sheridan not won victories at Atlanta and in the Shenandoah Valley that revitalized the Republican Party.[8]

Lee's military successes in 1862 and 1863 created a belief that independence was possible as long as the Army of Northern Virginia and its celebrated chief remained in the field. E. C. Boudinet, the Cherokee delegate to the Confederate Congress, captured the pervasive attitude toward Lee and his army in June 1864: "Perfect confidence is felt that Lee will whip the enemy as he always does—You wouldnt dream[,] if you should walk through town and see the self satisfied air of everybody[,] that a hostile army of 150000 men were almost in sight of town, on bloody thoughts intent."[9]

Lee's penchant for offensive strategy and tactics has come under heavy attack from historians over the past two decades. The Army of Northern Virginia suffered very heavy casualties in its celebrated triumphs during 1862 and 1863. Various scholars have argued that a more defensive conventional strategy or a guerrilla strategy would have conserved manpower, thereby enabling the Confederacy to prolong the war and perhaps exhaust Union will. Such analysis overlooks the fact that Lee's strategic and tactical aggressiveness suited Confederate expectations (and countered superior Union numbers). Civilians hungered for news of aggressive success on the battlefield, which conveyed a sense of progress toward independence. Their morale required the type of victories Lee supplied from the Seven Days through Chancellorsville, and without which the Confederacy almost certainly would have collapsed sooner.

In July 1864, surgeon Thomas Bailey of the Army of Tennessee reflected a widely held concern about generals who preferred defensive strategy and tactics. Joseph E. Johnston's withdrawal from northern Georgia to Atlanta left Bailey "more depressed" than ever before. "Will Johnston opt for retreat or a rush for victory? Or to let Atlanta fall without a struggle? These are questions asked again and again. But it is all centered on one man's power—General J. E. Johnston," observed a frustrated Bailey. Turning from his pessimistic talk of Johnston, Bailey spoke encouragingly about Lee, who had sent Jubal A. Early on an offensive through the Shenandoah Valley that eventually threatened Washington: "But why despair? Our sky is brighter in other parts of the Confederacy . . . If Robert E. Lee's strategy is successful, Sherman may be obliged to fall back."[10]

The Confederate military ultimately proved unable to win enough victories at crucial times to carry their nation to independence. Contrary to what much recent literature proclaims, defeat in the military sphere, rather than dissolution behind the lines, brought the collapse of the Confederacy. Lee's surrender at Appomattox convinced virtually all Confederates that their attempt at nation-making had failed. Having lost half of their white military-age population to death or injury and seen their social and economic systems ripped apart, they learned a bitter lesson in failure spared the vast majority of white Americans throughout more than two centuries of United States history.

The following chapters explore the themes of popular will, national sentiment, and military strategy during the Confederacy's brief existence. They offer a reading of Confederate history substantially at odds with some interpretations that currently hold sway. This is especially the case with Chapters 1 and 2, in which I suggest that scholarly preoccupation with the admittedly substantial evidence of discontent in the Confederacy has cast into the shadows the actions and attitudes of the majority of white southerners who supported the war. In chapter 3 I contend that the Confederacy could have won the war, and that Jefferson Davis and Robert E. Lee pursued strategies that, although unsuccessful in the end, held great promise and satisfied the temperament of the Confederate people. In all three chapters I call for greater attention to the myriad connections between events on the battlefield and morale behind the lines—and especially to the singular impact of Lee and his Army of Northern Virginia on Confederate resolve and national sentiment. In the final chapter I argue that Confederates believed they had been beaten on the battlefield rather than undone by internal divisions. Unhappy at the death of their slaveholding republic, they sullenly accepted northern triumph but sought to perpetuate memories of the Confederacy and of the men and women who had struggled, at frightening human and material cost, to give it life.

Because my arguments respond to prominent trends in the literature, each chapter includes some attention to historiography. But this is not primarily a historiographical survey. Discussion of earlier works serves as a point of departure to offer alternative views of the Confederate experience and to suggest areas of fruitful scholarly examination in the future.

....

Any historian who argues that the Confederate people demonstrated robust devotion to their slave-based republic, possessed feelings of national community, and sacrificed more than any other segment of white society in United States history runs the risk of being labeled a neo-Confederate. As a native of Los Angeles who grew up on a farm in southern Colorado, I can claim complete freedom from any pro-Confederate special pleading during my formative years. Moreover, not a single ancestor fought in the war, a fact I lamented as a boy reading books by Bruce Catton and Douglas Southall Freeman and wanting desperately to have some direct connection to the events that fascinated me. In reaching my conclusions, I have gone where the sources led me. My assertions and speculations certainly are open to challenge, but they emerged from an effort to understand the Confederate experience through the actions and words of the people who lived it.

1

POPULAR WILL

*"Many years yet I fear, we are to endure
these severe trials"*

The Confederate populace waged a determined struggle for independence. No other segment of white American society has persisted in any endeavor so destructive of human and physical resources. Yet despite an unparalleled level of loss, Confederates often have been judged wanting in devotion to their cause. Scholars have described in abundant detail waning Confederate morale and have speculated at length about why white southerners did not resist longer. They have argued that political dissension, class strife pitting the yeomanry against planters, doubts about the morality of slavery, fears that God favored the North, the absence of a shared sense of purpose, and other factors explain why the Confederate experiment in rebellion failed. For more than half a century, the overriding scholarly question almost always has been "Why did the Confederacy collapse so soon?" Not only have scholars usually failed to place the Confederate resistance within a comparative context of broader American history, but they also too often have slighted or ignored entirely an equally important question, namely, "Why did so many Confederates fight for so long?" Until the second question receives the detailed

....

17

attention long accorded the first, the history of the Confederacy will remain imperfectly understood.

Preoccupation with fissures within the wartime South arises from an understandable tendency to work backward from the war's outcome in search of explanations for Confederate failure. Historians begin with the fact that the North triumphed. Large and well-equipped Union forces remained in the field in April 1865. No apparent social upheavals rent northern communities as the armies played out the war's closing scenes at Appomattox, Durham Station, and elsewhere. After four years of conflict, the North seemed able to continue to fight the war and maintain social equilibrium, which has suggested to many historians a stronger northern will to win. What weaknesses in Confederate society, scholars have wondered, eroded southern will at a rate more rapid than that experienced in the North?

A book published for the American Historical Association in 1990 reflected the consensus of recent scholarship. "With slavery increasingly weakened by black actions, the Confederate government molded its policies to protect the interests of the planter class, and these policies in turn sundered white society," observed Eric Foner. "Many nonslave-holding whites became convinced that they bore an unfair share of taxation . . . Above all, the conscription law convinced many yeomen that this was a 'rich man's war and a poor man's fight' . . . The result, by 1863, was widespread draft resistance and desertion—a virtual civil war within the Civil War, which sapped the military power of the Confederacy and hastened its defeat." Foner mentioned "elements of opposition to the war" in the North but claimed, without amplification, they were "not as widespread as in the South."[1]

An unfolding panorama of social upheaval similar to that described by Foner dominates many scholarly writings about the wartime South. Bell I. Wiley observed in 1956 that "A cursory glance at the Confederacy reveals numerous instances of bitter strife, and one who delves deeply into the literature of the period may easily conclude that Southerners hated each other more than they did the Yankees." Internal division appeared before secession, noted Wiley, and "eventually became so intense it sapped the South's vitality and hastened Northern victory." E. Merton Coulter rhapsodized about southern soldiers and civilians who manifested "a feeling of loyalty and self-sacrifice for the common good" but lamented their insufficient numbers. It must have pained a neo-Confederate such as Coulter to reach his famous conclusion that the "forces leading to defeat were many but they may be summed up in this one fact: The people did not will hard enough and long enough to win." The four authors of *Why the South Lost the Civil War,* the most detailed examination to date of factors underlying Confederate defeat, agreed with Wiley and Coulter. "We contend that lack of will constituted the decisive deficiency in the Confederate arsenal," they wrote in 1986. "Confederates embarked on an enterprise demanding the utmost in teamwork, unity, and loyalty, without possessing these virtues in adequate degree. When the military effort began to falter, Confederates were unable to pick up the slack sufficiently to compensate for the loss of military strength."[2]

When did this lack of will reach crisis proportions? Many historians point to a surprisingly early date. Charles Grier Sellers, Jr., argued that the "first flush of enthusiasm was rapidly supplanted by an apathy and a growing disaffection which historians have identified as major factors in the Confederacy's failure." Bell Wiley thought "the turning point of the war probably came in the spring of 1862 rather than in July, 1863, the usually accepted time." Passage of the conscription act and suspension of the writ of habeas corpus, military defeats in the Western Theater, and a split between Jefferson Davis and the Confederate Congress all occurred in the first months of 1862. Looking at these events, Wiley termed it "apparent that the South's ability to wage war effectively was severely and permanently curtailed."[3]

The summer of 1863 is most frequently mentioned as the Confederacy's great divide. Malcolm McMillan's analysis of the Alabama home front detected after "Gettysburg and Vicksburg a defeatist attitude . . . that could not be reversed." Steven Hahn's study of a pair of upcountry Georgia counties—a work too often cited to make points about the Confederacy as a whole—agreed that "the South found its prospects dimming after the summer of 1863, when the Union won decisive battles at Gettysburg and Vicksburg." Only "determined resistance along with military engagement on favorable terrain" could have reversed Confederate fortunes after mid-1863, wrote Hahn in generalizing beyond his small corner of Georgia, and the Confederacy proved unable to muster the requisite effort because of class tensions that alienated its hill country folk and internal disagreement about the future of slavery. In a careful assessment of Jefferson Davis's role as president, Paul D. Escott also looked to the third summer of the war: "The defeats at Gettysburg and Vicksburg in July, 1863, represented severe blows to morale and led many soldiers and civilians to conclude that the war was hopeless." Economic distress and class antagonisms bedeviled attempts to shape a united southern defense, and, as 1864 dawned, Davis "had to spend much of his time fighting against disintegration." According to Bell Wiley, Gettysburg and Vicksburg cast a "cloud of gloom . . . over the land and the Southern spirit suffered an injury from which it never recovered."[4]

Historians emphasize internal fissures but disagree about what or whom to blame for the disaffection—a hopeless military situation, privations, disgust with self-centered planters, or other factors. Growing class friction dominates many explanations. Questionnaires collected from veterans in Tennessee during the early twentieth century implied an inevitable collapse of the Confederacy because small farmers and landless white people concluded that they had suffered enough in defense of slavery and vowed to sacrifice no more. Responses to the questionnaires also suggested that military service heightened class divisions because common folk in the ranks envied officers who lived better and "partook of the honor of command" and that a far smaller percentage of enlisted men than of officers remained committed to the war effort. A leading student of life in the armies argued that the experience of soldiering strengthened rather than weakened enthusiasm for the Confederacy, while still concluding that mounting evidence of class bias helped produce "a gradual withdrawal of support on the part of many southern whites."[5]

Planters and yeomen often seemed locked in a dialectic certain to scuttle Confederate hopes for independence. More concerned with property and standing than with Confederate success, the slaveholding elite demanded favorable legislation that alienated many yeomen. Among planters along the lower Mississippi River, observed a pair of able historians, "selfishness appears to have been their dominant trait, self-interest their only creed." Only early in the war—before any hardships hit the lower Mississippi—did these individuals manifest strong support for the Confederacy. Yeomen and poor people put up with such behavior for only so long. Squeezed by inflation and slighted by a government that seemingly did nothing to help families suffering in the absence of husbands and fathers in uniform, common folk deserted Confederate armies and the cause they served.[6]

A study of Washington County, North Carolina, sketched contentious classes motivated almost solely by economics. In a departure from other historians, Wayne K. Durrill described an initial alliance between planters and landless poor against middling farmers. But "landless unionists eventually turned on the county's yeomen and seized their lands as well as parcels belonging to planters." In choosing courses of action during the conflict, each of the planters, yeomen, and laborers "evidently did calculate how his own economic interests might best be served." Durrill observed—without offering specific figures on enlistments or the size of the military-age white population—that "local

....

volunteers did not flock to the Confederate cause. They had to be cajoled." Apparently generalizing from his one-county sample, he added, "Like small farmers and laborers in many parts of the South, they found this a rich man's war and a poor man's fight and believed the purpose in fighting was to secure the property of slaveholders." Regrettably, Durrill mustered only one letter to substantiate these sweeping claims, an evidential problem that plagued much of his analysis of the attitudes and actions of yeomen and poor whites.[7]

Durrill's book typifies a tendency to treat the Confederate yeomanry as a monolithic group. Do the yeomen of Hahn's two upcountry Georgia counties, Durrill's Washington County (an atypical area by almost any yardstick), and selected other sections of North Carolina reveal much about the behavior and beliefs of their counterparts across the Confederacy, from whose ranks came the vast majority of the soldiers who bore the brunt of the southern resistance? The answer must be a firm no. Elizabeth Fox-Genovese and Eugene D. Genovese have warned against the temptation to lump together upcountry, piedmont, and lowland yeomen. They suggest that most yeomen viewed black people with a similar blend of fear and hatred, but when it came to supporting the Confederacy patterns differed markedly between nonslaveholding residents of the upcountry and the plantation belt. Even within regions, the yeomen seldom presented a unanimous front. Until further work sheds light on additional geographical areas, generalizations about "the Confederate yeomanry" should be attempted only with caution.[8]

Women have not escaped attention in analyses of the disintegrating Confederate home front. Once again, the picture becomes dismal as the war moves beyond 1863. As selfish as the lower Mississippi's planters, elite women discontinued support for the Confederacy because it failed to protect their privileged status. Tensions flared between wealthy and less affluent women, and the latter lost their enthusiasm for a government that demanded heavy economic and personal sacrifice. Well before the war's third year had closed, women's initial patriotism had eroded under the pressure of human and material loss. A widely reprinted article by Drew Gilpin Faust portrayed Confederate women alienated by a government that could not protect them and ignored their interests. "Historians have wondered in recent years why the Confederacy did not endure longer," concluded Faust. "In considerable measure, . . . it was because so many women did not want it to . . . It may well have been because of its women that the South lost the Civil War." Another scholar averred that the loss of Vicksburg and heavy casualties at Gettysburg "cast down the sophisticated and naive alike." A belief that God would grant the Confederacy victory also weakened when buffeted by endless casualty lists and growing privations. By January 1864, a "crisis in theological confidence rooted in the earliest months of the war threatened to overwhelm the hardiest female patriots."[9]

Other historians echo these conclusions about the impact of religion on Confederate morale. Typical are the authors of *Why the South Lost the Civil War,* who stated that "defeat in battle and loss of territory cast doubt on whether God truly favored the Confederacy and, for those who concluded that God did not, the cause seemed hopeless." Thousands of Confederates wondered why they should fight on against God's apparent disfavor. "A powerful prop initially," concluded the authors, "religion thus became a source of weakness in adversity."[10]

Doubts about slavery have been put forward as a similarly baleful influence on Confederate morale. Forty years ago, Bell Wiley suggested that "uneasiness about slavery gnawed at numerous Southern consciences." Declining fortunes on the battlefield and in foreign affairs convinced many Confederates "that in clinging to slavery they were defying the moral sentiment of the world, and the consciousness of disapproval by Christian people everywhere made them extremely uncomfortable." Charles Sellers and Kenneth M. Stampp expanded on this theme in a pair of famous essays. Sellers insisted that thousands of white southerners were tortured by doubts concerning slavery because the institution "simply could not be blended with liberalism and Christianity . . . Forced to smother and distort their most fundamental convictions by the decision to maintain slavery, and goaded by criticism based on these same convictions, Southerners of the generation before the Civil War suffered the most painful loss of social morale and identity that any large group of Americans ever has experienced."[11]

Stampp found comparable guilt about slavery among Confederates. "A large number of white Southerners," he believed, "however much they tried, could not persuade themselves that slavery was a positive good, defensible on Christian and ethical principles." Many of these people believed that a Union victory with emancipation "would do for the slaveholders what even the more sensitive among them seemed unable to do for themselves—resolve once and for all the conflict between their deeply held values and their peculiar and archaic institution." Although he could assemble little direct testimony "to suggest that Southerners lost the Civil War in part because a significant number of them unconsciously felt that they had less to gain by winning than by losing," Stampp offered an array of what he termed "circumstantial evidence": Confederate political leaders argued among themselves about state rights and other issues to the detriment of the cause; civilians in areas occupied by the Union army failed to mount underground resistance of the type common in twentieth-century wars; and, "most significant of all, was the readiness, if not always good grace, with which most Southerners accepted the abolition of slavery." Following what Stampp considered a tepid war effort, ex-Confederates found reward in a defeat that provided the means "to rid themselves of the moral burden of slavery."[12]

On this point the authors of *Why the South Lost the Civil War* employed language and reasoning much like Stampp's. Confederates possessed an "essentially ephemeral allegiance to slavery" that eroded rapidly during the war. Lincoln's Emancipation Proclamation fanned existing embers of doubt about the institution and made many white southerners "even more uneasy about their isolation in a world in which the great powers of Europe, now joined by the United States, sought to extirpate slavery." Unable to bear the "weight of world moral disapproval," many Confederates abandoned their commitment to slavery—and with it a major reason to strive for an independent southern nation.[13]

The foregoing characterization of the Confederate will to win touches on elements of a scholarly consensus that has emerged over the past half century. Put simply, this consensus portrays supporters of the Confederacy as only superficially united at the outset of the conflict and quick to divide over a range of issues. By the middle of 1863 if not sooner, Confederate society had begun to unravel. The yeomanry and poor white people resented conscription, the tax-in-kind, impressment, and other governmental measures that seemed to fall harder on them than on the wealthy. Planters sought to safeguard their property and status to the detriment of national goals. Women suffered economically and increasingly questioned a patriarchal system that failed to protect their way of life. Initially a source of strength, religion became another part of the problem, and doubts about slavery surfaced as beleaguered white southerners surveyed a western world solidly in favor of emancipation. War weariness set in early, national morale plummeted, desertion and disaffection increased exponentially, and the Confederate resistance collapsed from internal stresses that rendered further military struggle impossible.

This scholarship has shattered the tenacious Lost Cause myth of a united Confederacy, but in doing so it has created new distortions. Historians employing the analytical prisms of class, gender, and race have focused almost exclusively on sources of division, and the resulting picture begs an obvious series of questions. If the situation had deteriorated so strikingly by the middle of 1863 or the beginning of 1864, why did so many thousands of yeomen, planters, and women continue to support the Confederacy for another one and a half to two bloody years? What were the factors that bound these people to the cause? Why did they resist the centrifugal forces that pulled others away from allegiance to the Confederacy? How did their level of effort and sacrifice compare to those of northerners and of other Americans in United States history?

After discussing internal weaknesses in the Confederacy for more than 400 pages, the authors of *Why the South Lost the Civil War* noted that "Confederates fought harder than Americans ever fought, or needed to fight, facing far more formidable opposition than Americans ever confronted, and without allies." Similarly, Steven Hahn admitted that, despite the "inherent contradictions and class conflict" he emphasized so strongly, "the Confederate nation managed to command sufficient social unity to struggle on for four years" because "backwoods farmers, sacrificing their lives in great numbers, . . . formed the backbone of the war effort and enabled the Southern armies to remain in the field as long as they did."[14] The unintended irony in such statements highlights the need to balance fruitful examinations of Confederate weaknesses with comparable attention to sources of strength and to provide at least some comparative context.

Would other Americans have fought as long and hard and at such enormous cost? This question cannot be answered, but a few statistics are instructive. The Confederacy mobilized between 750,000 and 850,000 men, a figure representing 75 to 85 percent of its available draft-age white military population (only the presence of slaves to keep the economy running permitted such an astonishing mobilization). At least 258,000 of them perished during the war (94,000 on the battlefield and 164,000 from disease), and those wounded in combat totaled nearly 200,000. Deaths thus ran to about one in three of all men in uniform, and killed and wounded in battle to between 37 and 39 percent. The North mustered at least 2.2 million men, about half of its 1860 military-age population, of whom 360,000 died (110,100 in battle and the rest from disease or accidents) and 275,175 were wounded. With a death rate of one in six, and killed and wounded in battle amounting to about 17.5 percent, the North paid a relatively much lower price in blood than the did the Confederacy.[15]

American combat losses in other conflicts drop off sharply from the Union figures. An estimated 184,000 to 250,000 colonists served during the American Revolution, of whom 10,500 were killed or wounded in battle—a rate of between 4.2 and 5.7 percent. During the War of 1812, the numbers were 286,730 serving and 6,765 killed and wounded in battle (2.4 percent); the war with Mexico, 115,874 and 5,885 (5.1 percent); the war with Spain, 306,760 and 2,047 (less than 1 percent); World War I, 4,743,826 and 257,515 (5.4 percent), World War II, 16,363,659 and 961,977 (5.8 percent); the Korean War, 5,764,143 and 136,913 (2.4 percent); and the Vietnam War, 2,600,000 and 201,000 (7.7 percent). The far higher rate of casualties in the Confederate military is striking. What cannot be known is how other Americans would have reacted to comparably high losses. What if there had been more than six million battle casualties in World War II? Or nearly a million in Vietnam? More to the point, how would northern society have stood up to battlefield losses exceeding 850,000 rather than 385,000?[16]

And what of material damage? The war cost the Confederacy two-thirds of its assessed wealth (much of that total was in slave property), killed 40 percent of its livestock, destroyed more than half of its farm machinery, and left levees, railroads, bridges, industry, and other parts of the economic infrastructure severely damaged or ruined.[17] How would severe shortages of basic goods have affected Union morale? What if Confederate armies had marched across the northern country-side, devastated large parts of key states, disrupted communications and transportation, and created scores of thousands of refugees? Again, such speculative questions cannot be answered, but Pennsylvania's anemic response to the presence of the Army of Northern Virginia in June 1863 suggests that northerners might have chosen not to make markedly greater sacrifices to win their war for union and emancipation.[18]

As it was, the North manifested all the symptoms of disaffection and war weariness scholars have discussed at length concerning the Confederacy. Union support for the conflict reached such a critical low point during the summer of 1864 that Lincoln wrote his famous memorandum stating, "This morning, as for some days past, it seems exceedingly probable that this Administration will not be re-elected." Throughout the war, significant numbers of northerners chafed at suspensions of the writ of habeas corpus, groused about taxes, hotly debated the issue of emancipation, and demonstrated violently against conscription. Nothing equivalent to the New York City draft riots of July 1863 occurred in the Confederacy. At least 200,000 northern soldiers deserted, and another 120,000 evaded conscription. One scholar estimated that "no less—and probably more—than 85,000 to 90,000 Americans in all fled to Canada during the war, either to dodge enrollers, to avoid the draft or to desert the army." Thousands more congregated in the mountainous counties of central and western Pennsylvania and elsewhere, where they lay beyond the easy reach of enrolling officers.[19]

Desertion by Confederate soldiers has been a main beam supporting the lack-of-will edifice, but its strength may be more apparent than real. The presence of Union armies on southern soil generated a type of Confederate desertion unknown among Union soldiers—and one that did not necessarily indicate weak will or unhappiness with the Confederacy. In a letter representative of a large body of evidence, a Georgia soldier in the Army of Tennessee informed his wife in mid-July 1864 that "a great many Tennesseeans and up[country] Georgians are leaving the army and say they are going back home . . . They know that their families are left behind at the mercy of the Yankees, and it is hard to bear." This man assured his wife that he and most of his comrades remained confident of final victory, but if the southern army retreated beyond his home county "and we were to pass on by you and the children, I could not say that I would not desert and try to get to you." Thousands of other Confederates left the ranks when they marched close to the areas where their families lived but later returned to their units. In her pioneering work on desertion, Ella Lonn estimated that

8,500 of 12,000 deserters from Virginia and nearly 9,000 of 24,000 from North Carolina rejoined the army. How should these men be categorized?[20]

At the least, historians should avoid portraying Confederate desertion as a linear problem of constantly increasing gravity. A recent study of the Old Dominion described a bulge of desertions in 1862 that probably represented anger at implementation of the Conscription Act, the terms of which extended the service of thousands of men who originally had signed on for one year. After this initial wave, rates dropped off until the final months of the war. "Virginia's experience," concluded William A. Blair, "calls for modification of explanations of desertion as demonstrating a lack of will to fight or identity with the Confederate cause." Similarly, Kevin Conley Ruffner's examination of desertion in the 44th Virginia Infantry contradicted the image of a steadily mounting problem. Ruffner found that most deserters left the 44th during the early period of the war, "a product of the recruitment of men unsuited for military life." At the end of 1864, a time when many historians have argued that desertion swept unchecked through southern armies, the 44th "had a desertion rate of less than 3 percent of its effective strength." A recent comparative study of the 24th and 25th North Carolina Infantry regiments concluded that an "overwhelming majority" of each unit's initial volunteers performed steadfastly throughout the war. The 25th suffered a much higher overall rate of desertion among replacement troops, however, "because of the instability and poor quality of its company-grade command structure."[21]

Union desertions cannot be attributed to enemy threats against northern civilians; neither is it likely that many Federals left the army because they believed their families were starving. For these reasons, northern desertion would seem more clearly to indicate loss of will or disaffection from the national cause than do the actions of thousands of Confederates who sought to protect families or left the ranks only temporarily. Even almost certain victory did not stop the problem of northern desertion, as indicated in a letter from the Petersburg lines a month before the end of the war. "The spirit of our army has very much improved, desertions less frequent than a short time since," wrote a Confederate posted near Hatcher's Run: "Yanky deserters still continue to come over."[22]

Because northern soldiers contended with fewer worries about the safety and material well-being of their families and stood a much better chance of avoiding death or wounds in battle, scholars should be careful about attributing to them superior morale. Reid Mitchell has observed that "the ideology and the morale of the Union soldier made a key contribution to Union victory; one reason the Union could triumph was the perseverance of its soldiers." On the Confederate side, Mitchell detected "ideological and structural weaknesses" that were "key to Confederate defeat." Bell Wiley quietly ignored evidence of serious disaffection among northern citizens and soldiers in stressing the "depth of the North's devotion to the Union." Even if Lee had won a victory at Gettysburg and captured Washington and other major northern cities, he wrote, "it seems extremely doubtful, in view of the North's devotion to the Union, that the outcome of the war would have been other than what it was."[23] Implicit in both Mitchell's and Wiley's statements is a belief that Confederate morale was less tenacious than that of the North; absent in both is any sense of the relative tests to which each side's morale was put—tests that should enter into any assessment of morale on either side.

Thousands of Confederates remained in the ranks during the last year of the war. Indeed, the size of the Army of Northern Virginia varied but little at the outset of each of the war's last three spring campaigns. In May 1863, Robert E. Lee faced Joseph Hooker at Chancellorsville with about 61,000 men. When Ulysses S. Grant's Federals crossed the Rapidan River the following May, Lee's army mustered 65,000. Just before he began his retreat to Appomattox in early April 1865, Lee defended the Richmond-Petersburg front with just fewer than 60,000 soldiers.[24]

Nor should modern readers assume the existence of some vast un-tapped reservoir of military-age white men in the Confederacy. At least three out of four went into the service. Thousands more labored in vital agricultural or industrial jobs. Still others could not serve because of legitimate physical disabilities. In the spring of 1864, the Conscription Bureau canvassed the Confederacy's manpower. This survey indicated that the draft had been "eminently successful" in Virginia, North Carolina, and South Carolina, but less so in Georgia, Mississippi, Alabama, and Florida. As for finding more men to place in service, the Bureau, in language so poorly worded as to frustrate easy understanding,

informed the secretary of war that "results indicate this grave consideration for the Government, that fresh material for the armies can no
longer be estimated as an element of future calculation for their increase,
and that necessity demands the invention of devices for keeping in the
ranks the men now borne on the rolls. The stern revocation of all
details, an appeal to the patriotism of the States claiming large numbers
of able bodied men, and the accretions by age, are now almost the only
unexhausted sources of supply." One sentence spoke eloquently to the
paucity of manpower and likely sent a shudder through Secretary of
War James A. Seddon: "For conscription from the general population,
the functions of this Bureau may cease with the termination of the year
1864."[25]

Events proved the accuracy of the Bureau's projections. "I have been
out soldiering, and have only returned to attend to such special business
as the secretary needed to have immediately done," a young man in the
War Department wrote to his aunt in October 1864. She had complained that two detailed men helping on her plantations would be
called away to military service. "The demand at present for recruits to
the Army is so great as to require the revocation of all details granted
by the Secretary of War," the nephew explained gently. "Every man
will be taken from our Department permanently, (they are out now as
local troops) except such as cannot possibly be dispensed with." He
understood this would work a "great hardship" on his aunt, but reminded her that "it cannot be as bad as being under Yankee rule—
What can be as bad as that!"[26]

A recent study of Greene County, Georgia, underscored how cleanly the Confederate search for manpower swept many southern counties. With an 1860 population of 1,075 white males aged thirteen to forty-five, the county sent 800 men into eight companies of regular infantry and cavalry and hundreds more into militia units. "Virtually all of the county's military-age males of all class backgrounds, plus many older men and some boys," concluded the author, "served in the Confederate armed forces or the militia during the war." Extensive analysis of 575 of these men from four regular companies yielded chastening figures: 173 (30 percent) died while in the service; another 81 (14 percent) were discharged as permanently disabled. Fourteen men were listed as official deserters, and one-quarter of the 141 present to surrender at Appomattox had received at least one wound during the war.[27]

Just as Confederate desertion should not be viewed as linear, neither should Confederate morale be charted in a gloomy curve declining toward Appomattox after the summer of 1863. A majority of the Confederacy's white population resisted long past the points at which scholars often suggest southerners believed there was little or no hope for victory. The period February–May 1864, for example, witnessed considerable optimism. A series of Confederate victories, which receive little attention now compared to larger battles such as Gettysburg and Vicksburg or Chattanooga, lifted southern spirits. Northern offensives failed in February at Olustee, Florida, and in early April at Mansfield and Pleasant Hill, Louisiana. Confederates under Robert F. Hoke captured Plymouth, North Carolina, on April 20, and Nathan Bedford

Forrest defeated Federals at Okolona, Mississippi, and captured a garrison of black soldiers and white unionists (many of whom were slaughtered after they surrendered) at Fort Pillow, Tennessee, in February and April respectively. "The spirit of the Southern Confederacy was scarcely ever more buoyant than in the month of May, 1864," remarked newspaper editor Edward A. Pollard in his *Southern History of the War*. Expectations of success were nearly universal, and in Richmond and elsewhere "the hope was freely indulged that the campaign of 1864 was to be the decisive of the war, and to crown the efforts of the South with peace and independence."[28]

Although Pollard painted too bright a picture, his statements accurately captured common sentiments. In late March, Atlanta's *Southern Confederacy* applauded the performance of southern soldiers "wherever our armies have been brought in contact with the enemy this spring . . . The courage and confidence of the people at home keeps pace, in the main, with that of the army, and they look forward hopefully to a bright and glorious future." In Richmond, the *Dispatch* warned against complacency arising from battlefield successes: "Although we are decidedly of the opinion that events, so far, have been such as to give us great hope for the future, we would not have our people grow over confident." Civilians should emulate the spirit of the soldiers, who realized "that they have before them a task of great difficulty. Yet they are not only willing but anxious to enter upon it." Richmond's *Enquirer* detected weakness in a North resorting to repeated drafts of balky conscripts: "The war spirit is broken, is gone, and indications of peace will soon crop out all over the surface of Northern society. Confederate victories this Spring will end the war spirit, and fully and completely develop the prospects of an early peace." The Charleston *Daily Courier* contrasted a depressing late 1863 with more propitious times in early 1864. "Never at any period of this bloody war has the spirit of soldiers and people been more in keeping with the character of the occasion than at the present time," it observed. Soldiers were resolutely shouldering their muskets, and "those outside the army are performing their duty to those noble men with cheerful alacrity and munificent generosity."[29]

Soldiers and civilians joined newspaper editors in projecting success for the Confederacy in early 1864. Seven witnesses struck typical chords. A Virginia cavalryman posted near Fredericksburg, Virginia, stated plainly, "We will certainly whip Grant if he does come." Reuben A. Pierson, a Louisianian serving in the Army of Northern Virginia, worried about reports of flagging morale in his home state. "Can it be that the noble and generous people of our State are ready to submit to the yolk of our oppresers?" wondered Pierson in a letter to his father. "Nothing is shurer than our ultimate success." He added, "Our army here is in the highest spirits and ready to meet the enemy at any day that we may be called on by our leaders." Pierson's "blood chill[ed]" at the thought "that I must forsake all my State pride; and look upon her as the only one that grew faint and despaired for want of true gallantry during the struggle for all that makes life endurable." A soldier writing to his wife from the battlefield at Mansfield gave a different impression of morale in Louisiana. "The Army and Citizens are in the highest Spirits that I have ever seen them," he exulted. "It is said that the gallantry and bravery of our army has not been surpassed by any army since the war began." A Georgian in the Army of Tennessee described morale in language similar to that used by Reuben Pierson regarding the Army of Northern Virginia. "I never saw the army in such fine spirits, everything is hopeful and confident since we repulsed them above Dalton," wrote A. J. Neal to his sister. Neal "anticipate[d] brilliant successes this spring and after a few hard fights a glorious victory."[30]

From his vantage point in the Confederate capital, war clerk John B. Jones tallied recent Confederate successes on April 30. "Federal papers now admit that Gen. Banks has been disastrously beaten in Louisiana," he wrote. "They also admit their calamity at Plymouth, N.C. Thus in Louisiana, Florida, West Tennessee, and North Carolina the enemy have sustained severe defeats . . . [T]he work of concentration goes on for a *decisive* clash of arms in Virginia . . . Our men are confident, and eager for the fray." Robert Garlick Hill Kean, another bureaucrat in Richmond, alluded to financial problems in the North that many Confederates interpreted as harbingers of Union failure: "Gold in New York 173½ at last advices and tending upward. Many hopeful indications of a general breaking up in the United States, political as well as financial." Kean believed that the next campaign in Virginia would decide the issue. A Georgia woman detected the hand of God behind good news pouring in from every front. "What gratitude should fill our hearts as Christians for all these evidences of divine mercy!" remarked Mary Jones. "And we can but hope the day of our deliverance from our wicked foes is drawing near. I have never despaired of the final issue, but I have never before felt the dawn of hope so near. I trust it is not a presumptuous delusion!"[31]

Although an increasingly somber mood permeated the Confederacy after the summer of 1864, expressions of hope and determination appeared frequently in letters and diaries well into the last year of the war. Soldiers—at least those in Lee's army—probably retained a stronger sense of possible victory than did many civilians, but ample testimony also suggests a persevering attitude behind the lines. Following Confederate debacles in the Shenandoah Valley in late fall 1864, one of Jubal Early's soldiers passionately, if somewhat awkwardly, declared that "every man woman & child ought in the face of God this day in the language of our forefathers . . . pledge their lives . . . & their sacred honor to the prosecution of this war . . . & summoning all our energy our resolution & our resources to that one object make the prosecution of this war the business of our lives." Two months later, a lieutenant in the 14th Georgia Infantry of the Army of Northern Virginia admitted that low spirits prevailed among many of his comrades but insisted that he had no intention of giving up: "We have got the whole Yankee armey yes the whole Yankee nation to fight but I am going to stay and fight as long as there is any Southern soldiers in the field."[32]

As the Army of Tennessee moved north toward Nashville in mid-

November 1864, a scene in Florence, Alabama, revealed an impressive bond between Confederate civilians and their soldiers. "Last Sabbath morning the citizens of Florence turned out en masse to witness the crossing of Stewart's and Cheatham's men over the Tennessee River," reported a soldier in the 37th Georgia Infantry. Men and women, young and old, and "the grave and the gay . . . lined the sidewalks and thronged the streets, to see and welcome the grand old veterans of the Army of Tennessee." Just a few days later, thousands of soldiers in these two divisions showed desperate courage in mounting some of the most impressive—and hopeless—assaults of the war against well-positioned Federals in the battle of Franklin.[33]

Many soldiers and civilians evinced a stoic resolve to fight on no matter what the toll. Even Lincoln's almost certain re-election, which would deal a major blow to hopes for southern independence, failed to convince numerous Confederates that the end was at hand. "Our party is sending on its last men," wrote a member of the 1st South Carolina Cavalry on the day northerners cast their votes for president. A landholder who owned ten slaves and cultivated about 100 acres, this man declared: "We are putting forth our utmost strength, & I much fear that we will not be able to hold out much longer. But if our army can get supplies of provisions, we will fight them to the last rather than be subjugated." Following the northern presidential canvass, staff officer Francis W. Dawson of James Longstreet's corps addressed a surge of Union optimism triggered by Lincoln's re-election. "Of course the Yanks think they are going to close up in a very short time," he wrote with more optimism than the South Carolina cavalryman had been able to muster, "but they know not as we know the pride and power of the South." Dawson believed that the South could continue the fight for at least two more years—and "at any cost in preference to surrendering that fair land to the tyrannous rule of the North." Spirits remained high in the army and among civilians, and "no one thinks or dreams of subjugation."[34]

The failure of a peace mission headed by Vice President Alexander H. Stephens in February 1865 prompted many Confederates to review the Confederacy's options. A Texan in Lee's army welcomed Stephens's failure because he believed it would spur Confederates to greater exertions. "And now I reckon . . . the peace men, women, and children will cease to talk so much in regard to it, as all hopes for such are blasted, until won by our own earnest efforts," wrote William M. Baines of the 4th Texas Infantry. "There is no use in talking or wishing for peace," Baines continued. "We cannot get it until won upon the field of battle. As for me, I would rather fill a soldier's grave, side by side with my many brave and devoted comrades upon the fields of Old Virginia, than to return to those who are more dear to me than even life, a whipped and degraded soldier." Baines proclaimed the Confederate cause a just one and predicted that "the Lord will give us peace and independence before a great time." A Georgian writing to her daughter shared Baines's determination. "So there remains only the alternatives, war to the bitter end or subjugation," stated Sallie Bird in reference to Stephens's effort. She pronounced the Confederate people "resolved not to submit, and so this cruel, this interminable, this ferocious war goes on. More hearts are to wail, more blood [is to] be shed, and the end is beyond the reach of mortal ken. Everyone sees the fact and braces himself for the danger."[35]

A veteran of nearly three years in the army had predicted an equally difficult future the preceding December. "I am afraid this war is bound to last another term of four years or perhaps until the South is subdued or the [Southern soldiers] and men or Yanks exhausted," stated John Wood to his father. Although "very tired of this war" and longing to be home, Wood added bravely that "It will take the North several years to conquer the South if she ever does." Susan Emiline Jeffords Caldwell of Warrenton, Virginia, took a similar view in late March 1865. "Many years yet I fear, we are to endure these severe trials," she confessed to her husband. Although she had lost a daughter during the war, seen her home plundered by Federal soldiers, and witnessed substantial devastation in Warrenton and Fauquier County, Caldwell remained committed to the war: "I want peace but I don't want to go back into the *union*. I want *Independence* and nothing else.—I could not consent to go back with a people that has been bent on exterminating us." Writing from South Carolina five weeks before Lee's surrender, Captain Jared E. Stalling also alluded to Union outrages. "The conduct of the enemy during the war has fully demonstrated to us what will be our miserable condition in case of subjugation," he observed. "The Confederacy is now straining the last nerve for its existence, and needs the services of every man at least who bears arms."[36]

Such testimony should caution historians against overemphasizing the admittedly impressive evidence of disaffection and disillusionment from the summer of 1863 forward. Although literary evidence may be biased toward the more patriotic groups, notably men and women of the slaveholding class who had the most to lose should the Confederacy fail, the actions of soldiers and glimpses of the yeomanry behind the lines indicate a complex mood of deepening gloom punctuated by desperate bursts of hope. Anyone seeking to gauge the state of Confederate morale during the last two years of the war must guard against equating war weariness with lack of will or indifference toward the fortunes of the Confederacy. Virtually all Confederates (and northerners) wished for peace by 1862, and those wishes grew more intense as slaughter on the battlefield and sacrifice on the home front escalated. But on what terms did most war-weary Confederates hope for peace? A mass of testimony suggests that many of them intended to fight on toward victory and southern nationhood.

Thus could Tully Francis Parker, an officer with the 26th Mississippi Infantry in Lee's army who desperately missed home and longed to see his wife and children, write in May 1864: "I am getin very Tyred of this way of Living but such is the fate of *war* and I know no better way than to Try to be Reconciled to our fate . . . I am not by any means willing to yield to the federal government and surrender." The previous March a similarly war-weary Sergeant Abram Hayne Young of Joseph B. Kershaw's brigade had reaffirmed his belief that "our Government is good" and that, if well provisioned, the Army of Northern Virginia would continue the struggle. "There is non hoo have boore more of the hardships," he asserted in reference to Lee's soldiers, "and are still willing to endure them rather than Submit to Such men as are Seeking to destroy us and all we have . . . [W]e are not near whiped."[37]

A pair of well-known women's diaries exemplify the phenomenon of war-weariness combined with resolve to continue the struggle. Kate Cumming looked back on 1864 as a year that left "much coveted peace seemingly as distant as ever" and the Confederacy "drenched with the blood of martyrs!" Beseeching the lord not to "turn thy face from us, and save, O, save us from this terrible scourge," Cumming next sounded a defiant note: "Although woe and desolation stare at us every way we turn, the heart of the patriot is as firm as ever, and determined that, come what may, he will never yield." Some Confederates had abandoned hope, acknowledged Cumming, "but, thank the Giver of all good, they are in the minority." South Carolinian Emma Holmes heard rumors on April 22, 1865, that Lincoln had been assassinated and peace negotiations begun "that would reconstitute the Union much as it had been (even with slavery likely intact) if the Confederates would fight the French." Much as Holmes desired an end to the killing, she could not countenance the thought of peace without independence: "To go back into the Union!!! No words can describe all the horrors contained in those few words . . . We could not, we would not believe it. Our Southern blood rose in stronger rebellion than ever and we all determined that, if obliged to submit, never could they *subdue* us."[38]

Determining the extent of southern white guilt about slavery poses difficulties similar to separating pervasive war-weariness from genuine despair or indifference about the Confederacy's prospects. Kenneth M. Stampp has written that in spite of white southerners' "defense of the kind of slavery that existed among them and denial of its abuses, many of them, as their unpublished records eloquently testify, knew that their critics were essentially right." But direct evidence that sizable numbers of Confederates harbored serious doubts about the morality of slavery is scarce, and much of the other evidence put forward by historians has been inferential or open to alternative interpretation. For example, both Stampp and Bell Wiley quoted a letter from Frederick A. Porcher to Judah P. Benjamin in late 1864. "Is it not manifest that it is this chasm [slavery] which has withheld from us the sympathy and cooperation of the great powers of Europe?" asked Porcher. "Are we not fighting against the moral sense of the world? Can we hope to succeed in such a struggle?" Was Porcher, who did not concede the superiority of the world's moral sense on the issue, feeling guilt about slavery or simply discomfort at the thought that its presence harmed the Confederacy's chances for independence?[39]

Wiley also mentioned Robert E. Lee as a Confederate who deplored slavery and likely experienced pangs of conscience. Alan T. Nolan has laid to rest the notion that Lee was antislavery (Lee's partisans have denied Nolan's arguments with tenacity reminiscent of the Lost Cause writers), and the general's own comments indicated that his willingness to embrace gradual emancipation stemmed from a desire to strengthen the Confederate war effort rather than from moral guilt. When the Confederate debate over arming slaves arose in the winter of 1864–65,

Lee wrote that he considered "the relation of master and slave, controlled by humane laws and influenced by Christianity and an enlightened public sentiment, as the best that can exist between the white and black races while intermingled as at present in this country." He went on to say that because of the North's superior manpower (enhanced by former Confederate slaves who served with the Union army) the South should arm slaves and give them benefit of "a well-digested plan of gradual and general emancipation." Emancipation certainly would "occur if the enemy succeed," Lee continued, so "it seems to me most advisable to adopt it at once, and thereby obtain all the benefits that will accrue to our cause." Three years later, while president of Washington College, Lee remarked that he had told Jefferson Davis "often and early in the war that the slaves should be emancipated, that it was the only way to remove a weakness at home and to get sympathy abroad, and to divide our enemies, but Davis would not hear of it."[40]

Studies of slavery in Confederate states similarly fail to support the picture of pervasive guilt. Clarence L. Mohr detected "moral qualms about slavery" among some white women in Georgia but concluded that much of their expressed guilt "reflected concern over the breakdown of slave discipline and revulsion at the harsh measures being used to keep blacks in subjugation." In wartime Tennessee, John Cimprich found that most white people "struggled desperately" to retain slavery: "The institution did not die quietly but screaming and clawing for survival." Stephen V. Ash's portrayal of life in the occupied Confederacy also suggested tenacious efforts to maintain the institution in the face of pressures from the Union army and from slaves striving to break free of their bondage. Union victory confirmed emancipation, but a brutal lesson carried over from the years of occupation: "To whites throughout the occupied South, the lesson was plain: the more violence they were able to inflict on blacks, the more thorough was their racial mastery. It was a lesson they had seen confirmed countless times in the past and would see confirmed again and again in the years to come."[41]

Indeed, for every statement such as Mary Chesnut's famous "ours is a *monstrous* system and wrong and iniquity" (which itself attacked not the institution of slavery but the practice of white men exploiting slave women as mistresses and thus degrading white women), many others can be marshaled to indicate unquestioning support for slavery. In her perceptive study of women on southern plantations, Elizabeth Fox-Genovese demonstrated that "the complaints of slaveholding women never amounted to a concerted attack on the system, the various parts of which, as they knew, stood or fell together." Elsewhere Fox-Genovese put the matter more bluntly: "In recent years, a wide array of scholars has viewed slaveholding women as secret—or not so se-cret—opponents of a slave system that purportedly oppressed them as thoroughly as it oppressed black slaves. This dubious view may absolve the women of the Old South of the sins of slavery, but it does little to enhance our understanding of the commitment of white southerners, women as well as men, to slavery as a social system."[42]

Typical of strongly proslavery sources are the diaries of Eliza Francis Andrews and Catherine Ann Devereux Edmondston. Andrews lamented in early 1865 that "this glorious old plantation life should ever have to come to an end." Ten weeks later, in reaction to discussion about freeing slaves in the Confederacy, she bridled at the specter of forced abolition via Union military power: "To have a gang of meddlesome Yankees come down here and take them away from us by force—I would never submit to that, not even if slavery were as bad as they pretend." Andrews thought that an independent Confederacy should confiscate "the negroes of any man who was cruel to them, allowing them to choose their own master . . . this would make it in everybody's interest to treat them properly." Edmondston recorded her thoughts on the subject as 1864 drew to a close. The Confederacy should never arm and free black men, she asserted, because "we have hitherto contended that Slavery was Cuffee's normal condition, the very best position he could occupy, the one of all others in which he was happiest . . . No! freedom for whites, slavery for negroes. God has so ordained it."[43]

Edmondston's reference to divine approval of slavery raises the question of whether religion sapped or bolstered morale as the war progressed. As with so many aspects of the larger topic of Confederate will, the contemporary written record provides something for everyone. What it does not provide—at least not until the very last days of the war—is any clear-cut sense that most southern white people believed they should abandon the struggle because God had forsaken their cause.

Throughout 1864 and into 1865, many Confederates viewed their travails as orchestrated by a deity who eventually would reward their efforts with success. "We feel that our trials are but for a season, and are purifying us," observed a Virginia woman in January 1864, "and we shall come out of this war a glorious people, fighting our own battles, independent of any other nation." Writing three months later, a private in the 12th Virginia Cavalry admired Lee's generalship and lauded the Army of Northern Virginia—"no General ever had such an army as he"—but believed "the God of Battles is to decide the mastery in the approaching contest." Cut off from his family, who lived well behind Union lines, this man affirmed that "though in the past three years He has suffered us to be sorely tormented and aliens to occupy our lands and strangers our houses, He never brought us so far in that struggle to turn us over to the tender mercies of the enemy." Exuding even more optimism about providential favor, one of James Longstreet's staff officers averred in late April 1864 that "God has certainly blessed our armies this year. Whenever we have met the enemy—in S.C., Fla., Miss., Tenn., Ky., Va., La., and N.C., the victory has been ours, with apparently very little effort on our own part."[44]

Devout soldiers often equated duty to God with duty to the Confederacy. "This was a covenant that could not easily be compromised or abandoned, especially when God seemed to be testing his people with misfortune on the battlefield," observed Peter S. Carmichael in his biography of artillerist William Ransom Johnson Pegram. In March 1865, less than a month before he was killed at the battle of Five Forks, Pegram sought to reassure his family. "He has his good purpose in chastising us now," wrote the young battalion commander, "which, I doubt not, when it is revealed to us, we will find to have been to *our good.*" Brig. Gen. Stephen Dodson Ramseur of North Carolina shared Pegram's religious fervor and steady faith in victory, urging his brother-in-law in October 1864 to resist the temptation to become discouraged. "Let us be brave and cheerful and trustful," he implored. "Dont give up. We are bound to succeed. The God of Justice will order all things for the good."[45]

Two Virginians and a South Carolinian in Lee's army specifically yoked duty to God and to country as the spring campaign of 1864 approached. "I cannot but think that if we are true to ourselves and do our whole duty," wrote F. Stanley Russell of the 13th Virginia Infantry, "that a just and almighty God will crown our efforts with success and peace. Our people are beginning to rely solely on God and themselves for success—they have ceased to look to Europe, the outside world for support." Lieutenant Ted Barclay, whose 4th Virginia Infantry served in the Stonewall Brigade, seconded Russell's sentiments: "Our cause we believe to be a just one and our God is certainly a just God, then why should we doubt." Barclay's sister should "confidently expect a glorious issue in the impending campaign, a campaign between right and wrong . . . the struggle will be a bloody one, but it is noble to die in so just a cause."[46]

Samuel C. Clyde of the 2nd South Carolina Infantry assured Hattie Crook of Greenville, South Carolina, that God's spirit was at work among Lee's soldiers in ways that would help bring Confederate independence. While visiting a Mississippi brigade, Clyde had counted about

150 men at the altar during one of "the most glorious revivals I ever witnessed. I came away after the benediction, leaving them still singing, shouting & praising God." Comparable religious sentiment pervaded the army, and he expected a bright future: "Very many of our brave defenders are enlisting under the 'blood stained banner of the Cross of the Captain of our salvation.' The Christian soldier is praying, the ministers of God are laboring. In short, the followers of the Lord Jesus are engaged in a mighty struggle with Satan and his wicked legions, and I am happy to add, are victorious in every conflict." Because of those victories, stated Clyde, "We look for glorious times soon."[47]

Revivals of the type described by Clyde swept through the southern armies periodically, most notably between the winter of 1863–64 and the autumn of 1864, encouraging, as one historian put it, "a belief in God's providence [that] helped them endure the final months of agony before the Confederacy collapsed." George Cary Eggleston wrote after the war that these revivals helped inspire a "superstitious belief that Providence would in some way interfere in our behalf." This in turn contributed to "a sort of gloomy fatalism" that led to "singularly reckless" behavior in battle. Officially designated days of fasting and prayer appear to have been solemn occasions, widely observed by civilians and soldiers. Behind the lines, an indeterminate number of Confederates clung to an expectation of God's intervention until the very end. As Lee's army abandoned Richmond on April 2, a British observer described women unprepared for the grim news. "They cannot believe it—Heaven will interfere. it can never be!" recorded Thomas Conolly in his diary. "The long pent up tide of Emotions bursts forth & the poor girls fling themselves on down on their sofas & chairs & weep & sob 'till their hearts seem breaking." From occupied New Orleans, Sarah Morgan resisted tears at news of Lee's surrender. "Every body cried," she confided to her diary, "but I would not, satisfied that God will still save us, even though all should apparently be lost."[48]

On the day of Lee's surrender at Appomattox, Union Col. Charles S. Wainwright exhibited a curious lack of fulfillment. For three years the Army of Northern Virginia had "withstood every effort of the Army of the Potomac; now at the commencement of the fourth, it is obliged to succumb without even one pitched battle." Wainwright would have preferred to end the war with a smashing Union victory such as Gettysburg. "As it is," he concluded, "the rebellion has been worn out rather than suppressed."[49]

Wainwright's analysis was perceptive. The Confederacy had sputtered to an end under intense military and economic pressure applied by the armies of a powerful and confident North. Many thousands of Confederate citizens had long since lost heart, their society showing the strains of disaffection, desertion, and class tension. Doubts about slavery or fear of God's disfavor plagued at least some white southerners, causing them to turn their backs on the Confederacy. But most yeomen and planters, men and women, old and young had continued to support the Confederate resistance until well into 1864 or beyond. No other white Americans have lost such a huge percentage of their young men killed or maimed, or have had to withstand such intense pressures for so long.

Scholars need to explain why so many Confederates fought so hard. Elizabeth Fox-Genovese and Eugene D. Genovese have noted that nonslaveholding yeomen proved "loyal enough to allow the South to wage an improbable war in a hopeless cause for four heroic years."[50] The dramatic but debatable allusion to hopelessness aside, this passage highlights a crucial truth too often lost in the historical literature. What motivated the loyal Confederate yeomanry? What motivated the slaveholders who fought alongside them? Only satisfactory answers to these questions will balance the impressive body of work on components of Confederate failure and give a more complete picture of the Confederate will to win.

In reaching conclusions about the steadfastness of southern white morale, historians must keep in mind comparative contexts. They might look to the observations of a pro-Union French correspondent, who, in a long piece written for the Paris newspaper *Le Temps* in early September 1864, offered a keen analysis of the two societies at war. Confederates had faced "bankruptcy, despotism, famine" and "no longer have anything to hope for except independence; they no longer have anything to lose except their life." This man found honor in "the courage that they deploy in this long resistance" and heroism in "this obstinacy of a common people who, for two years, block[ad]ed, invaded, decimated, found resources, [and] faced immense forces from the Union." The Confederate economy lay in ruins "from top to bottom; all able men from fiteen to fifty-five are under arms . . . One no longer sees but women in the families and Negroes in the fields."

Yet Confederates manifested discipline born of "a unity of will" and still "held on, and no one can say when they will succumb."

Northern society presented a vastly different picture. The North "has not renounced its richness," stated the Frenchman, "the war has interrupted neither its industry, nor its commerce." Daily life progressed essentially as in peacetime, and northerners shrank from "extreme measures, acting little and spending a lot, placing mercenaries opposite seasoned men, wasting immense resources without breaking down a poor enemy." The Union effort lacked the sense of collective direction evident in the Confederacy. Writing before the full impact of Sherman's capture of Atlanta had become evident, this correspondent perceived a potentially disastrous lack of will above the Potomac: "The North can yield to fatigue; then the war would have served only to substitute a national hate for a political rivalry; and to ruin more profoundly the Union."[51]

In many ways, Louisa May Alcott's *Little Women* captured the degree to which the war disrupted daily life in the North—the March girls miss their father while he is away in the army, but otherwise their days proceed much as before the conflict. Few areas of the Confederacy could claim such a tranquil setting after mid-1862. This essential difference and its implications for popular will and morale should inform any analysis of the southern war effort.

A fuller picture of how morale changed over time and across regions will yield a greater understanding of the Confederacy. There may have been generational differences between men and women reared during the bitter sectional debates of the late antebellum years and those who grew to maturity in less contentious times. It may be possible to sort out the hard-core deserters from those who returned to service after leaving the army, the bitter opponents of the Confederacy from those who expressed unhappiness with specific Confederate policies but still wanted southern independence.

Many historians have stressed material deprivation and class tensions fueled by a sense that wealthier people had access to more goods and sacrificed less than poorer Confederates. All too often, analysis has consisted of little more than applying a crude formula wherein increased privation equals growing disenchantment. This overlooks the fact that common suffering can produce greater resolve to oppose those causing the physical distress. By the end of 1863, prolonged resistance against an enemy with seemingly unlimited manpower and industrial capacity had created among many Confederates a sense of accomplishment against long odds and a determination to carry on the fight. As the pro-administration Richmond *Dispatch* proudly announced in April 1864, the Yankees, according to their own newspaper accounts, had sent more than two million men against the Confederacy, created a 600-ship navy, occupied much southern territory, and built an unparalleled industrial war machine—all "without producing the slightest disposition to succumb, or in the remotest degree shaking the firm and confident faith" of the Confederate people. Although the *Dispatch* attributed too little impact to the Union effort, its basic point merits close attention.[52]

William Tecumseh Sherman, who scrutinized the Confederate nation as he prepared for a new military campaign in the spring of 1864, would not have disputed the *Dispatch*'s conclusions about the state of southern morale. The spectacle of white southerners still apparently devoted to winning independence after three years of hard conflict prompted a perceptive assessment by the North's master of psychological warfare. "The devils seem to have a determination that cannot but be admired," wrote Sherman to his wife on March 12, 1864. "No amount of poverty or adversity seems to shake their faith—niggers gone—wealth and luxury gone, money worthless, starvation in view within a period of two or three years, are causes enough to make the bravest tremble, yet I see no sign of let up—some few deserters—plenty tired of war, but the masses determined to fight it out." Sherman's subsequent actions and statements underscored his belief that severe measures would be necessary to break the dogged Confederate resistance.[53]

Historians typically have emphasized only religion and guilt about slavery as nonmaterial factors that affected Confederate morale, portraying both as ultimately destructive. But what of the ideology and ideals, which bolstered Confederate will to varying degrees throughout the conflict, and the interplay between beliefs and material circumstances? James M. McPherson discussed these issues in his preliminary study of Confederate soldier motivation: "The concepts of southern nationalism, liberty, self-government, resistance to tyranny, and other ideological purposes . . . all have a rather abstract quality. But for many

Confederate soldiers these abstractions took a concrete, visceral form: the defense of home and hearth against an invading enemy." Confederate definitions of freedom and liberty may not accord with modern ones, but they resonated at the time and helped keep men in the ranks and foster support behind the lines.[54]

The relative importance of military and nonmilitary influences on fluctuations in morale has not been clearly defined. There has been a good deal of interest in how disaffection behind the lines promoted desertion and how the presence of deserters in turn exacerbated problems on the home front. Unfortunately, the ways in which campaigning armies hardened civilian will have garnered far less attention. Most scholars have assumed that northern incursions into the Confederacy dampened southern enthusiasm for the war. In fact, the Union army probably had the opposite effect on many Confederates, acting as a catalyst for muting grievances about issues such as the tax-in-kind, impressment, and the draft. When the question came down to accepting heavier economic burdens and greater governmental infringement on personal liberty or submitting to Yankee soldiers who had killed thousands of their men and wreaked havoc on their society, many Confederate civilians chose the former.

The single greatest factor engendering Confederate hope after the midpoint of the war was trust in Robert E. Lee and the Army of Northern Virginia. Lee's stunning victories between June 1862 and May 1863 created a mystique that lasted until the final stage of the war. The Army of Northern Virginia expected to win, and its confidence radiated to a populace conditioned to expect bad news from all other military theaters. Lee and his soldiers ascended to a position comparable to that occupied by George Washington and his Continental army during the American Revolution. For thousands of Confederates, they personified the Confederacy; in Marse Robert and his army, rather than in Jefferson Davis and the government, resided southern hopes for victory. Because of the immense symbolic value attached to the Army of Northern Virginia, southerners and northerners alike believed its surrender marked the end of the war—despite the continued presence in the field of other major Confederate forces.

One thing seems certain amid all the unanswered questions about the Confederate resistance. Many thousands of white southerners developed feelings of allegiance to a cause that transcended locality and narrow interests. But did those feelings constitute nationalism? Did Confederates fight primarily to defend home ground and family, or did the possibility of establishing a new slaveholding republic figure prominently in their actions? In short, what was the relationship between popular determination to defeat northern invaders and loyalty to the idea of a Confederate nation?

The Sumter Light Guards of Americus, Georgia, photographed in Augusta while en route to Virginia in April 1861. Hundreds of thousands of men volunteered for Confederate service during 1861–62, and more than 80 percent of the military-age white men of the Confederacy eventually donned uniforms. The steadfast service of the vast majority of these soldiers, often against long odds, constituted the most impressive evidence of strong popular will in the Confederacy. (Library of Congress)

Several hundred women in Richmond, Virginia, took to the streets on April 2, 1863, to protest high prices and shortages of food. Widely reprinted in modern literature, this northern image graphically supports the idea that the Confederacy suffered from an erosion of will and was unraveling from within by the midpoint of the conflict. (*Frank Leslie's Illustrated Newspaper,* May 23, 1863)

Although less compelling than the image of protesters in Richmond, this wartime depiction of women making clothes for Confederate soldiers illustrates a far more common scene of domestic support for the troops. Thousands of Confederate women sent a steady stream of clothing to men at the front. In his letters to Mary Custis Lee, Robert E. Lee frequently noted shipments of socks: "I received dear Mary last evening the bag of socks & your note of the 18th," he wrote during the spring of 1864. "The count held out this time, 43 pairs. I sent them to the Stonewall Brigade which I heard were in need . . . I have sent out to ascertain who are in need to be prepared for the next arrival." (Library of Congress)

ROBBING THE CRADLE AND THE GRAVE.

This northern cartoon, titled "Robbing the Cradle and the Grave," portrays a southern woman sending her father and infant son off to the Confederate army: "Well, father, you've got to go, I see," reads the caption. "Jeff Davis had better take little Pete along too. You'd both be jest the age for two soldiers." Although meant to lampoon the Confederate war effort, it indicates that the North understood the remarkable degree to which the South mobilized its human resources. (*Harper's Weekly,* December 17, 1864)

On April 12, 1864, black soldiers at Fort Pillow, Tennessee, were slaughtered by Confederates under the command of Nathan Bedford Forrest. A cause célèbre in the North, this incident remains one of the most controversial of the war. Fort Pillow was one of several small victories, often overlooked in modern considerations of Confederate morale, that bolstered southern will during the late winter and early spring 1864. (*Frank Leslie's Illustrated Newspaper,* May 7, 1864)

A northern sketch of Sherman's soldiers looting a South Carolina farmstead in 1865 suggests an almost carefree attitude on the part of at least some of the men. Throughout the war, destruction of this type tested Confederate will in a manner not experienced in the North. (Paul F. Mottelay and T. Campbell Copeland, eds., *The Soldier in Our Civil War: Columbian Memorial Edition. A Pictorial History of the Conflict, 1861–1865,* 2 vols. New York: Stanley Bradley Publishing Co., 1893, 2:300)

The presence of large armies quickly exhausted an area's food and fodder, often leaving its residents in desperate condition. In this engraving, Confederate women accompanied by two slaves make their way to a Union commissary to request rations. As in the case of physical destruction of property, shortages of food challenged but did not destroy Confederate will. (*Frank Leslie's Illustrated Newspaper,* November 28, 1863)

Confederate civilians came under fire on many occasions, a dimension of the war virtually unknown in the North. This sketch depicts Charlestonians scattering as a Union shell bursts. The Charleston *Mercury* reported on December 28, 1863: "The Christmas of 1863 will long be remembered by those who passed the day in the city of Charleston . . . At one o'clock a.m., the enemy opened fire upon the city. Fast and furiously were the shells rained upon the city." (*Harper's Weekly,* January 9, 1864)

Federal shelling of towns and looting of houses and businesses often stiffened Confederate resolve to fight on toward independence. On December 11, 1862, Fredericksburg, Virginia, anticipated the experience of many other Confederate cities when a Federal artillery bombardment left many of its streets littered with ruined buildings. (Francis Trevelyan Miller, ed., *The Photographic History of the Civil War,* 10 vols. New York: Review of Reviews, 1911, 9:315)

A wartime sketch of northern soldiers ransacking homes and businesses in Fredericksburg the day after the bombardment. Union General Marsena R. Patrick described the scene: "When I went into the town a horrible sight presented itself—All the buildings more or less battered with shells, roofs & walls all full of holes & the churches with their broken windows & shattered walls looking desolate enough—But this was not the worst—The Soldiery were sacking the town! Every house and Store was being gutted!" (Library of Congress)

Discussions of Confederate morale often neglect to offer comparative context. The New York City draft riots of July 1863, during which more than 100 people perished, represented an outburst of domestic violence unmatched by anything that transpired in the Confederacy. This contemporary engraving shows police battling rioters near the office of the New York *Tribune.* (*Harper's Weekly,* August 1, 1863)

PENNSYLVANIAN GRATITUDE

The anemic response among Pennsylvanians to Lee's invasion in 1863 provides another point of comparison with Confederate reactions to far more protracted and destructive incursions by Union armies. Pennsylvania's failure to rally more resolutely to the national cause provoked angry comment in the North, as suggested by this cartoon titled "Pennsylvanian Gratitude." In the caption, an "able-bodied Pennsylvanian" demands payment from a thirsty New York soldier for a glass of water. "What's the good of having you fellows here from New York," asks the Pennsylvanian, "if we can't make something out of you to cover what we lose by the rebel raiders?" (*Harper's Weekly,* July 11, 1863)

This young soldier killed just a few days before Lee abandoned the Richmond-Petersburg lines in April 1865 speaks to the tenacity of Confederate will—as well as to how the Confederacy expanded its definition of "military-age men" in order to keep armies in the field. (Francis Trevelyan Miller, ed., *The Photographic History of the Civil War,* 10 vols. New York: Review of Reviews, 1911, 3:289)

2

NATIONALISM

"The Army of Northern Virginia alone, as the last hope of the South, will win the independence of the Confederacy"

Strong feelings of national identity helped spawn the impressive will Confederates exhibited during their war for independence. With the goal of mounting the broad military effort necessary to establish nationhood, soldiers and civilians of the Confederacy tolerated severe intrusions on personal freedom, accepted the erosion of state rights as the central government sought to equip and feed its armies, and, toward the end, debated openly the possibility of arming and freeing slaves to win the war. Their letters and diaries referred to "my country," "our nation," "the South," "our independence," the "southern people," and otherwise reflected national identification and purpose. Robert E. Lee and his soldiers functioned as the principal focus of Confederate nationalism for much of the war, and young slaveholding officers who had matured during the 1850s stood out as perhaps the most highly nationalistic component of the Army of Northern Virginia. Through battlefield victories, reenlistments, and letters to the home front, the officers and men of Lee's army served as an engine propelling national loyalty among civilians and soldiers throughout the Confederacy. The resulting sense of shared striving for independence in turn bolstered morale during trying periods. Testimony from April and May 1865 leaves no doubt that when Lee surrendered his army, many Confederates deeply mourned the death of their four-year-old republic.

Scholarly literature often has slighted the extent to which white southerners identified with one another as Confederates and looked forward to living in a country untrammeled by political interference from the North. Historians usually have discussed this topic within the framework of nationalism, asking such questions as: Did the Confederacy develop true nationalism? If so, how strong was it? How long did it last? Disagreement about how to define nationalism has characterized the debate, and too many scholars have pointed to disaffection in the Confederacy or to the fact of Union triumph as proof that white southerners never developed a national identity. The American experience in Vietnam inspired dubious comparisons of the Confederate and North Vietnamese struggles for independence, which inevitably used the Vietnamese victory to judge Confederates wanting in national purpose.[1]

Important questions concerning Confederate nationalism too often have gone unasked. What elements of the population exhibited a stalwart sense of collective loyalty to the Confederacy (as opposed to loyalty to a state that happened to be among the seceding states)? Why did they do so? Did Confederates look beyond their political leaders and government institutions for national identity and inspiration? Overall, those interested in Confederate nationalism have trained their lenses too exclusively on the government and civilians—an obsession with the home front that obscures the profound importance and influence of the armies, and especially of Lee, the Army of Northern Virginia, and the officers who led its regiments, brigades, and divisions. Similarly, students of the military side of the war have accorded too little attention to the ways in which the armies helped promote and sustain nationalism. As with so much Civil War literature, the gulf between scholars investigating the battlefield and those exploring the home front has hindered understanding of the innumerable ways in which the two spheres influenced and reacted to each other.

This gulf is especially vexing because of the obvious parallels between the roles played by George Washington and his army during the American Revolution and by Lee and his army during the Confederacy's fight for independence. Both generals led national armies that became symbols for their respective causes. Both contended with sagging civilian morale, disaffection among soldiers, and selfishness on the part of individual states or colonies. Both eventually eclipsed political leaders as national rallying points. Both relied on officers in their armies to help inspire civilians as well as soldiers. The importance of Washington and the Continental Army to emerging American national sentiment has received far more attention than the Confederate counterpart—perhaps because Washington and his army won their new nation while Lee and his did not.[2]

Writings on Confederate nationalism typically emphasize structural factors, ideology, or a combination of the two.[3] Some historians have pointed to political and military institutions and the growth of central power as evidence of Confederate nationalism. Typical was Frank E. Vandiver, who, in words reminiscent of William E. Gladstone's famous speech at Newcastle in October 1862, argued that "by late summer 1862, the Confederacy existed in its armies, in its emissaries, and in the hearts of its people—there was a Confederate 'nation.'" Faith in national success had sprung from Stonewall Jackson's campaign in the Shenandoah Valley and Robert E. Lee's victory over George B. McClellan in the Seven Days battles, producing "easy obedience to Confederate laws, acceptance of Confederate promissory notes, affection for soldiers and administrators." Emory M. Thomas, a student of Vandiver's, echoed his mentor in observing that "the Richmond government was characterized by centralization and nationalism." Conscription, suspension of the writ of habeas corpus, governmental control of industry, impressment of goods, and other such measures represented "manifestations of Confederate nationalism." By 1864–65, maintained Thomas, "the Confederacy had become for many Southerners an end in itself. The war experience had molded Southerners and defined them as a people."[4]

Drew Gilpin Faust is one of several historians who have explored ideology rather than structural or institutional manifestations of Confederate nationalism. Faust suggested that the "creation of Confederate nationalism was the South's effort to build a consensus at home, to secure a foundation of popular support for a new nation and what quickly became an enormously costly war." Religion supplied the overarching framework for southern nationalism, as Confederates cast themselves as God's chosen people. Concerns about greed (as manifested in hoarding, speculation, and profiteering) and the need to make slavery an institution compatible with biblical strictures dominated a debate over how best to forge a Confederate republic worthy of God's blessing. Faust noted the centrality of slavery to the Confederate consciousness: "As in antebellum defenses of human bondage, Confederates saw more at stake than mere political or economic self-interest. Slavery became, in both secular and religious discourse, the central component of the mission God had designed for the South." What scholars should not do, Faust warned, is work backward from Appomattox and yoke discussions of nationalism to those about why the Confederacy failed. Faust's own conclusions, however, stressed the ultimate weakness of nationalistic sentiment in the southern republic.[5]

The arguments of historians who find little evidence of true Confederate nationalism usually parallel those used to prove an absence of will, highlighting class conflict, government policies that failed to serve nonslaveholding interests, absence of unique cultural bonds, and doubts about slavery. These scholars often concede an incipient Confederate nationalism early in the first year of the conflict but insist that once Confederates got past the heady summer of 1861, with victory at First Manassas fading and the likelihood of significant sacrifice looming, the sense of national striving dissipated rapidly. Thus Paul D. Escott, while admitting that superior Union military power played a crucial role, stressed that Confederate nationalism "also foundered upon the tensions and contradictions of a class system that could not sustain both aristocracy and democracy during a severe crisis." By 1863 or 1864 at the latest, remarked Escott, "most Confederates knew the feeling voiced by one bitter farmer: 'The sooner this damned Government [falls] to pieces the better it [will] be for us.'"[6]

Unhappiness with the Richmond government among Confederates pursuing narrow class interests has figured prominently in a number of studies. An examination of Mississippi planters by Lawrence N. Powell and Michael S. Wayne found that "well before the end of the war the Confederate nationalism of the planters of the lower valley had ceased to have any functional meaning." Explicitly equating nationalism with morale, Powell and Wayne asserted that both "began eroding as the central government in Richmond encroached upon states rights prerogatives" and disappeared almost entirely when the national government "began to take on a life of its own (as governments tend to do) and placed its own survival above the concrete interests of the planting class." Escott similarly detected selfishness among a Confederate elite stubbornly insistent on protecting its own economic and social position: "The planters themselves proved to be contentious and narrow, unimaginative and inflexible, and only weakly committed to southern nationalism."[7]

The authors of *Why the South Lost the Civil War* noted that the growth of a strong central government constitutes evidence of one type of nationalism but argued that another variety held the key to Confederate failure. "This nationalism does not refer to a style of government policy or economic organization but to the emotional bonds between citizens of the would-be nation," they stated. "The problem, in a nutshell, is that the people of the South had no widely accepted mystical sense of distinct nationality." Only a belief in slavery and state rights united white southerners in 1861, and the Confederate government threatened both with conscription, impressment, and other policies as the war went on. Doubts about the morality of slavery functioned as a corrosive agent as the war progressed, leaving Confederates bewildered about their national goals. Kenneth M. Stampp previously had asserted that only slavery gave the South "a clear national identity." Pronouncing the idea of a distinct southern culture "largely a figment of the romantic imaginations of a handful of intellectuals and proslavery propagandists," Stampp claimed that most Confederates suffered few pangs of loss when their effort to create a new nation collapsed. Like the authors of *Why the South Lost the Civil War,* Stampp found in Appomattox and its aftermath proof of the fragility of Confederate national sentiment: "After Appomattox the myth of southern nationalism died, remarkably soon."[8]

More than thirty years ago, David M. Potter cautioned historians against "using the attribution of nationalism as a valuative device." Are "a people" rebels or patriots? Are they seeking independence or engaged in an insurrection? "When the historian attributes nationality to any group," wrote Potter, "he establishes a presumption in favor of any acts involving an exercise of autonomy which the group may commit; when he denies nationality, he establishes a presumption against any exercise of authority. The attribution of nationality therefore involves a sanction—a sanction for the exercise of autonomy for self-determination." A scholar who addressed both culture and common interest as components of national sentiment, Potter believed that the valuative implications of nationalism sometimes led "the historian to deny nationality to groups of whom he morally disapproves"—a perfect example of which would be the slave-based society of the Confederacy. "To ascribe nationality to the South is to validate the right of a proslavery movement to autonomy and self-determination," stated Potter. Few twentieth-century historians proved willing to do this, and their moral position sometimes "impelled them to shirk the consequences of their own belief that group identity is the basis for autonomy."[9]

The aroma of moral disapprobation envelops most arguments denying the existence of Confederate nationalism that have appeared since Potter issued his warning. Historians have found it very difficult to concede that the wish to preserve a society ordered by the institution of slavery could inspire pervasive national attachments. The authors of *Why the South Lost the Civil War* observed that many southerners left the Union "not because they shared a sense of unique nationhood but because they had a mutual fear of a society without slavery and white supremacy." Kenneth M. Stampp believed that by virtually replicating the United States Constitution in their own founding document (except for the latter's explicit protection of slavery, of course) and by laying claim to the American revolutionary heritage, Confederates "confessed rather pathetically the speciousness of southern nationalism."

Reid Mitchell concluded that a robust nationalism failed to develop in the Confederacy primarily because of one overwhelming weakness that was both structural and ideological—"the fact that the Confederacy was created as a means to defend racial slavery." For other historians, the absence of nationalism protruded most boldly from the Confederate landscape in the form of a selfish planter class seeking to protect its investment in human chattel regardless of the impact on its nation or fellow citizens.[10]

As with the question of will among white southerners, the currently dominant thinking about Confederate nationalism assumes a high point early in the war (if ever), followed by a steady dissipation beginning in the months following First Manassas and continuing to Appomattox. Too often historians identify an absence of nationalism as both cause and symptom of Confederate failure. The Confederacy lost because its people never developed a true sense of nationalism—or the Confederate people never developed a true sense of nationalism; if they had their struggle would have been determined enough to achieve independence. Many works that posit an absence of Confederate nationalism overlook or minimize two salient points. First, Confederates by the thousands from all classes exhibited a strong identification with their country and ended the war still firmly committed to the idea of an independent southern nation. Second, although these people finally accepted defeat because Union armies had overrun much of their territory and compelled major southern military forces to surrender, that acceptance should not be confused with an absence of a Confederate identity.

A precise breakdown of how many Confederates did or did not develop and maintain strong feelings of national identity lies beyond the reach of historical sources and methodology. The conclusions and quotations in this book were drawn from the letters and diaries of more than three hundred men and women.[11] As always, the paucity of testimony from the yeomanry and from poorer Confederates frustrates efforts to speak confidently about them—although the steadfast military service of scores of thousands of men from those groups certainly implies impressive ties to their country. Members of the slaveholding class left a far richer literary legacy, which, together with testimony from nonslaveholders and the actions of men and women from all ranks of society—whether serving in the military, complying with the onerous material demands of the central government, or otherwise sacrificing for protracted periods—suggests widespread and tenacious devotion to the Confederate nation.

Assuming that strong national identity existed in the Confederacy, I seek to convey the character of nationalistic sentiment as expressed in the letters and diaries of representative soldiers and civilians. Further, I argue that for many white southerners Robert E. Lee and the Army of Northern Virginia came to embody Confederate national identity after the second year of the war. Finally, I suggest that the generation of young slaveholding men who matured during the 1850s may have been among the most ardent Confederates, a cohort whose enthusiasm and fiery example probably enhanced feelings of nationalism within the armies and among civilians.

Brief attention to definitions and scope is in order before proceeding. I judged expressions such as "our country" or "our nation," which connote collective loyalties transcending state and locality, to be evidence of Confederate nationalism (if a writer used "my country" to refer to a home state, I did not use that reference as evidence of *Confederate* identity or loyalty). When alluding to country or nation, most Confederates meant a slave-based social system that guaranteed white control over the black people who made up 40 percent of the population. Confederate loyalty sprang from various sources, among them hatred for a foe who menaced the freedom and liberty, as well as the families and property, of most white southerners, and a belief that they shared cultural values at odds with those prized by northerners. Evidence of discord in the North also fed Confederate nationalism, rousing support for a sustained effort that many white southerners believed would expose the shallowness of northern commitment to sacrifice for the Union.[12]

Military service intensified feelings of national loyalty in two ways. For civilians with loved ones fighting hundreds of miles from home, it broadened their horizons and led them to think nationally as well as locally. For the soldiers, it inspired a belief that they sacrificed more for the cause than any other Confederates.[13] Subject to daily disruption of their normal lives and periodically confronted with the dangers of combat, soldiers rightly saw themselves in the vanguard of the struggle for independence. They often used language highlighting national purpose when writing either just before or after battles—in the former instances predicting that the upcoming clash might bring independence nearer, in the latter either affirming that victory had advanced the Confederacy's aspirations or, in the case of a defeat, expressing continued resolution to fight on for the Confederacy and its people.

Testimony from three men in the aftermath of Lee's victory at Fredericksburg in mid-December 1862 fits the second of these three patterns. The glad tidings of Christmas "proclaiming 'peace on earth, good will toward man,'" observed North Carolinian John F. Shaffner, "mingle with those which declare the triumph of *liberty, independence,* and *country.*" A member of the Rowan Artillery informed his cousin four days after the battle that the army had turned back "an effort on the part of the Yankees to destroy our nationality and every thing else that belonged to Southron institutions. But they have failed and I am happy to say they signally failed." Brig. Gen. Elisha Franklin Paxton of the Stonewall Brigade sounded a subdued yet confident note: "Our independence was secured in the last campaign when we proved our capacity to beat the finest army they could bring in the field," he wrote his wife. "The war may be protracted, there is no telling how long; but we have shown our capacity to beat them, and we are better able to do it now than ever before."[14]

Despite the pervasive image of horrendous Confederate desertion during 1864 and 1865, most soldiers discharged faithfully their military duty. Greater administrative control through provost marshals and other agents undoubtedly helped to keep men in the ranks (communities often assisted the government; had they not done so, it would have been virtually impossible to combat desertion), but dedication to the idea of an independent Confederacy and a sense of reciprocal obligation to others who sacrificed for the cause also contributed significantly to soldier loyalty.

Testimony from early 1864, as the fourth season of military campaigning approached, contains plentiful evidence of Confederate patriotism. A sergeant in the 45th Georgia, who had not seen his wife and son in more than fourteen months, expressed common sentiments: "I want this war to end and to be at home as bad as anybody can, but I do not believe I could enjoy myself at home in such times as these if I was able to do duty. Others would be fighting for their Country and My Country and home while I would be skulking my duty, and it would render me miserable." That same spring, a young Texas officer in Virginia confessed to his mother, "Oh! how I long to be at home more and more . . . and I hope that day will soon come." But he could not leave the army until "the fight is fought & the victory won." The army was confident, and his wish was that "our Noble Country having won its independence [may] be long blessed with peace." More effusive was Lt. Alexander G. MacArthur, who wrote while on watch the night of March 5, "I boast not when I say the country could not be in more secure hands than the soldiers . . . Such love of country and devotion to cause History furnished no parallel, as shown and proven beyond contradiction by the soldiers of the South. The ladies also."[15]

Many southern women matched the most committed men in their avowals of Confederate patriotism. Lamentations about a seemingly endless war, complaints about myriad hardships, and disgruntled letters to the secretary of war about conscription, material shortages or intrusive government agents—all of which have been cited endlessly by historians—should not be taken to mean most Confederate women jettisoned nationalistic feelings well before the end of the war. Considerable testimony presents a very different picture in which women not only placed the Confederacy above their own personal concerns but also expected their families to follow suit. When William Mason Smith triumphantly announced to his mother in April 1864 that a 60-day medical furlough made him "a free man for a while," he quickly received a stinging rebuke. "I am sure the Board was right not to send you back to the field," wrote his mother, "but you are wrong in the idea that their action makes you 'a free man.' You are *bound* by the duties of your position, & can only be 'free' when you conscientiously perform them . . . [Y]our time belongs to your Country & not to your pleasures . . . I hope you will not need the whole 60 days." Heeding his mother's instruction, Mason returned to his unit in time to be wounded at Cold Harbor; two months later he was dead.[16]

Other women expressed Confederate loyalties in varying ways. Tennessean Belle Edmondston sounded a familiar theme as she anticipated another year of war on New Year's Day 1864. "God grant successful may be the termination of 1864," she wrote. "Oh! my savior I have buried the past. Guide and leade me from temptation. After you God, then I live for my Country. God bless our leaders in Dixie." Later that spring, a young Virginia woman confessed a wish that every man who worked against the government could be executed. "They are our greatest enemies," she noted bitterly, "more dangerous by far, tha[n] those with whom we are at war— . . . [L]et every man help to protect his Country, & not rend and lacerate her by internal discords." Susan Emiline Jeffords Caldwell of Warrenton, Virginia, a town often occupied by Federals, reacted angrily in April 1864 to rumors of disloyalty among ladies in that community. "We are all loyal—we are very peculiarly situated and no people would do even as well as we do in the midst of an enemy," she wrote her husband. "We keep *true* to the South amid all our sore trials—and at times are to be pitied," she continued, revealing the special frustrations of those caught behind Union lines: "To have the enemy around you and come in and take your horses, your meat, corn & wheat at their pleasure and compelled to submit quietly."[17]

More striking yet was a petition to Secretary of War James A. Seddon from twenty-eight women of Harrisonburg, Virginia, in December 1864. They had watched with mounting anger as Philip H. Sheridan's army overpowered Jubal A. Early's defending Confederates and laid waste to the countryside in their part of the Shenandoah Valley. "With the permission of the War Department we will raise a full regiment of ladies—between the ages of 16 and 40—armed and equipped to perform regular service," read the petition. These women proposed "to leave our hearthstones—to endure any sacrifice—any privation for the ultimate success of our Holy Cause." A young South Carolina woman echoed this determination in April 1865. With only Joseph E.

Johnston's army between her and the legions of Grant and Sherman, Emma LeConte insisted that Jefferson Davis should call out the women to fight. All measures should be taken "that will give us freedom and not force us to live with such people—to be ruled by such horrible and contemptible creatures—to submit to them when we hate them so bitterly."[18]

Such statements confirmed attitudes evident among Confederate women from the beginning of the war. During the autumn of 1862, British visitor W. C. Corsan was so impressed with female patriotic ardor that he commented on it prominently in an account of his trip. Corsan understood—as many later historians did not—that physical privation and the loss of loved ones in the military often reinforced rather than eroded loyalty to the Confederacy. Because "the struggle has been prolonged and aggravated, until there is scarcely a family in the South which has not lost one or more of its number," he observed, the conflict "has become a war for independence—a war to save their soil from confiscation, and themselves and their families from poverty and insult." A number of Confederate soldiers told Corsan that they had cut short their furloughs because women "won't let a man capable of carrying and handling a rifle stay round home. If he can walk he must be off." Commitment to victory among women also helped guarantee the success of the draft: "It is this feature of the national feeling which makes the vigorous conscription in force at the South tolerable and effective."[19]

The experience of living under Federal occupation often deepened women's antipathies toward their foe. In New Orleans, Corsan noted that while "the Northern Conqueror is hated cordially by every class of residents," Confederate women were less guarded than men in their statements. He quoted one "pretty Creole lady" who readily revealed her venomous attitude toward soldiers occupying the city: "Oh! how I hate the Yankees!" she said belligerently: "I could trample on their dead bodies and spit on them!" In early 1863 from behind Union lines near Hampton, Virginia, Ann E. Hope reassured an aunt of her increasing devotion to the Confederacy: "Tell Sissy . . . she must not think because I am down here with the Yankees that I have turned Yankee. I grow stronger Southern every day[.] I am sertainly a Rebel, Rebel is the rightious name that Washington bore and why should not we have the same." Jane Howison Beale of Fredericksburg, Virginia, mocked invading Federals who expressed surprise at the absence of more union-ist sentiment in her community. Labeling them "profoundly ignorant of the moral science of causes and effects," Beale explained that "all history—all human experience teaches that those who suffer the tyr-anny of unjust warfare, learn to cling with a devotion to their principles that they would never have felt under milder influences and our Southern people will not be apt to form the first exception to this general rule."[20]

The example of women's patriotic steadfastness under duress inspired Confederate men throughout the war. A soldier in the Army of Ten-nessee denounced speculators and other evidence of corruption in Atlanta but applauded the "constant and glorious patriotism and self-sacrificing devotion to our cause" of the city's women—"the only redeeming virtue of the place." Robert E. Lee similarly praised the Confederate loyalty of women driven from Fredericksburg by a Federal bombardment prior to the battle in December 1862. Cast out of their homes into an unforgiving winter landscape, these refugees trudged westward toward relative safety. "I have only seen the ladies in this vicinity when [they were] flying from the enemy, & it caused me acute grief to witness their exposure & suffering," Lee informed his daughter Agnes. "But a more noble spirit was never displayed anywhere. The faces of old & young were wreathed with smiles & glowed with happiness at their sacrifices for the good of their country. Many have lost everything." Confederates from various parts of the nation echoed Lee's praise for the women of Fredericksburg and contributed thousands of dollars to relief funds set up within the Army of Northern Virginia and in several communities. "Let no man pretend to rejoice at the victory," wrote one newspaper editor, "who does not do his part in this work of benevolence." British observer Corsan, traveling in Virginia at about this time, also commented about the women's support for the war. "The women, especially," he noted, ". . . burn with an unquenchable thirst for revenge and victory."[21]

Confederate children also learned to be patriotic and mindful of their nation's needs. A Florida teenager recorded that on days set aside for fasting, humiliation, and prayer her father prescribed light meals for his children. "Eat sparingly, but do not refrain entirely," he admonished, "for if you do you will not be capable of the best work, and that is what our country calls for now." A Virginia father who had lost a seven-year-old son in 1863 instructed the next oldest boy "to study hard to fit himself for whatever place he may be destined to fill, that he may live not for himself alone but for his country." This man's thirteen-year-old daughter took to heart injunctions to place national welfare above personal consideration. "How I do wish dear Papa could be with us," she wrote in mid-June 1864, "although I would not like him to leave the army now. Of course we feel anxious about him, but I trust to 'Him who doeth all things right.'" A surgeon from Texas cast his thoughts toward future remembrance of the fight to create a new nation, sending home gold coins to be fashioned into stars similar to the ones he wore on his uniform. "They will do for our children as heirlooms," he told his wife, "to remind them of the part I took in the struggle for our country's independence and their liberty."[22]

Nothing better illustrated the existence of national loyalty than the debate over Confederate emancipation. Most supporters of arming and possibly freeing some slaves undoubtedly believed the plan would apply to only a small part of the southern slave population; they sought independence with slavery largely intact. That white southerners chose to discuss the issue at all reveals an attachment to the idea of an independent Confederacy so strong they were willing to tamper, at least to a degree, with their basic social structure. As Raimundo Luraghi cogently observed, "It is all too easy to scorn the Confederacy because it offered emancipation when it was almost doomed; one has only to think that slaveholders were speaking of *their own* expropriation, and that very rarely in history has an exploiting class ever arrived at such a degree of intellectual independence and self-denial." A careful student of the debate noted that "Jefferson Davis, Robert E. Lee, Judah Benjamin, and a host of less famous Southerners displayed greater flexibility about and willingness to begin modifying slavery than most accounts have ever admitted." It is worth noting that the Confederate Congress almost certainly never would have voted to arm slaves unless it perceived at least tacit approval among a majority of slaveholders. Lee's public endorsement made the congressional decision possible, a critical factor that underscored the general's status as the Confederacy's most important national figure. For pertinent comparative context, modern readers should look to the heated wrangling in the North about emancipation. Democrats and a few conservative Republicans excoriated Congress and Lincoln for the Second Confiscation Act, the Emancipation Proclamation, and other measures during 1862 and 1863—though slave property of loyal citizens was not at risk. It is easy to imagine the firestorm that would have accompanied any attempt in the North to tamper with the property holdings of a significant element of society.[23]

A majority of Confederate soldiers probably supported the idea of arming slaves—and not, as some accounts would have it, simply because they hoped to be replaced by black troops. However grudgingly, they went along with the proposal because they considered it a necessary condition to win independence. Indeed, Confederate veterans may have mounted scarcely more resistance to enrolling black soldiers in 1865 than their northern counterparts had manifested toward raising black regiments for the Union in 1862 and early 1863. "The army is passing resolutions favoring putting in the negroes & declaring their [own] determination to fight it out," wrote a Georgia officer in February 1865. The soldiers of the 49th Georgia Infantry similarly expressed their willingness to fight alongside black men: "When in former years, for pecuniary purposes, we did not consider it disgraceful to labor with negroes in the field or at the same work bench," remarked the regiment's company officers in summarizing attitudes among the men, "we certainly will not look upon it in any other light at this time when an end so glorious as our independence is to be achieved." Maj. Gen. John B. Gordon, who headed Stonewall Jackson's old Second Corps, informed Lee in late winter 1865 that "the officers and men of this corps are decidedly in favor of the voluntary enlistment of the negroes as soldiers . . . The opposition to it is now confined to a very few, and I am satisfied will soon cease to exist in any regiment of the corps." Gordon recommended that this information be "immediately forwarded to the authorities in Richmond."[24]

Self-interest and the cause of Confederate nationhood intersected in some arguments favoring black soldiers. Not only would such a step bolster the South's military forces, but it also would prevent a social and economic calamity likely to accompany Union victory. More than a year before the Confederate Congress took up the debate seriously, the Jackson *Mississippian* warned that failure to address the issue would be disastrous. "If Lincoln succeeds in arming our slaves against us, he will succeed in making them our masters," stated the *Mississippian*. "He will reverse the social order of things at the South. Whereas, if he is checkmated in time, our liberties will remain intact; the land will be ours, and the industrial system of the country still controlled by South-ern men." The proper course lay in the government's thwarting Lin-coln by taking immediate "steps for the emancipation or liberation of the negroes itself. Let them be declared free, placed in the ranks, and told to fight for their homes and country." By elevating continued white control of social and economic institutions above retention of the institution of slavery, the *Mississippian* probably articulated a view held by many nonslaveholders who supported the idea of recruiting soldiers from among the slave population.[25]

Some historians have chosen to highlight opposition to the govern-ment's endorsement of arming black men in the spring of 1865, espe-cially among the planter elite, as evidence of an absence of nationalism. The prospect of slaves in Confederate uniforms certainly did provoke angry criticism from the slaveholding community, but many of these critics nonetheless remained intensely loyal to the Confederacy—a fact usually omitted from discussions of their conduct during the debate. For example, a North Carolina planter's wife asserted in January 1865, "Slaveholders on principle, & those who hope one day to become slaveholders in their time, will not tacitly yeild their property & their hopes & allow a degraded race to be placed at one stroke on a level with them." Yet this woman's diary for the remainder of the war exuded loyalty to the Confederacy, including this passage written on April 16: "What is it that sustains me? . . . [I]t is faith in the *country.*

Faith in the *Cause,* an earnest beleif that eventually we will yet conquer! We cannot be defeated." Overall, the debate over arming slaves seems to have prompted a good deal of anger toward the government without diminishing appreciably determination to continue the struggle for Confederate independence.[26]

Many citizens of the Confederacy persevered in their national determination because of Robert E. Lee and his Army of Northern Virginia. By the midpoint of the conflict Lee and his men had become the preeminent symbol of the Confederate struggle for independence and liberty. Often preoccupied with Jefferson Davis and government institutions, historians interested in Confederate nationalism have failed to analyze Lee and his army as critical agents that engendered unity and hope. "The responsibility for fostering commitment to the nation fell to Jefferson Davis," wrote one scholar, "who, as a determined but distant personality, was both well and poorly qualified for the task." Early in the war, Davis "nurtured the frail spirit of nationalism with skill[,] . . . organized a government and articulated an ideology that avoided potential disagreements." Before a year had passed, however, Davis's efforts yielded diminishing returns, and by the beginning of 1864 the "administration was struggling against disintegration." Similarly, the authors of *Why the South Lost the Civil War* alluded to formal political structures in stating that the "Confederacy functioned as a nation only in a technical, organizational sense." Civilians and soldiers alike lacked deep national affiliations because the Confederacy "was created on paper, not in the hearts and minds of its would-be citizens."[27]

The written record contradicts this last assertion and affirms incontrovertibly that Lee and his soldiers influenced Confederate hearts and minds. From every state in the Confederacy, thousands of relatives, neighbors, and friends worried about the well-being of men in the army and cheered their successes. Apart from these ties, Lee's widely applauded Christian humility, bonds through marriage and ancestry to George Washington and other heroes of the American Revolution, and daring maneuvers as a commander struck emotional chords among fellow Confederates. Honorable, gallant, and audacious, Lee closely fit his people's ideal model of leadership. His army's string of victories afforded tangible proof of southern military prowess and prompted even skeptics to believe it possible to achieve victory and independence. From the surrender of Forts Henry and Donelson in the grim winter of 1862 to the near destruction of the Army of Tennessee in the fall and winter of 1864, a virtually unbroken stream of depressing news reached Confederates from the Western Theater. At the same time, Union naval forces inexorably tightened the blockade, hopes for European intervention dwindled, and shortages of various material goods plagued the beleaguered populace. The achievements of Lee and his army stood in spectacular contrast to this otherwise dreary picture. The Seven Days, Second Manassas, the invasion of Maryland and capture of Harpers Ferry, Fredericksburg, and Chancellorsville lifted Confederate spirits and elevated the Army of Northern Virginia and its commander to a position of national admiration and trust.[28]

Well before the close of the war, Lee and his army had come to embody the Confederacy in the minds of many white southerners. The piety of Lee, Stonewall Jackson, and other leading generals, as well as the revivals that swept the army's camps in 1863 and 1864, stirred the patriotism of Confederates who conceived of their nation as God's republic. The grit of yeomen who performed prodigious feats on numerous battlefields cheered all who wished to see Yankee invaders smitten. As faith in Davis and the political structure weakened, belief in Lee and his army grew, countering the divisive effects of politics, suffering, and defeatism. The national strivings of the Confederacy came to center on the army in Virginia, which, in winning victories and repelling numerous Union advances, nourished collective pride and confidence among soldiers and civilians. This is not to say Confederates outside Virginia ignored military operations elsewhere; they followed events closer to home avidly, while keeping a hopeful eye on the Eastern Theater. Jefferson Davis appreciated the vital part Lee and his army played, assuring the general following Gettysburg that a few critics could not "detract from the achievements which will make you and your army the subject of history and object of the world's admiration for generations to come."[29]

Testimony about Lee's stature within the Confederacy abounds. A Lynchburg newspaper called him "the central figure of this war" after Chancellorsville, praising his "calm, broad military intellect that reduced the chaos after Donelson to form and order." A British officer who traveled through nine Confederate states in the spring and summer of 1863 recorded that "no man has so few enemies, or is so universally esteemed. Throughout the South, all agree in pronouncing him to be as near perfection as a man can be." In the summer of 1864, a North Carolina woman rhapsodized: "What a position does he occupy—the idol, the point of trust, of confidence & repose of thousands! How nobly has he won the confidence, the admiration of the nation." Amid bad news accumulating from every quarter of the Confederacy in March 1865, a young South Carolinian asked, "Where is our Ray of hope?" The answer lay in Virginia, because "only to Gen. Lee and his poor little half-starved army can the people look—yet an army that has never suffered defeat, a contrast to the Western army." Even after the fall of Richmond in early April 1865, people took heart from Lee's presence at the head of his soldiers. "Happy is it for us that our Commander possesses the love & Confidence of the whole nation," wrote Mary Washington Early on April 4; "I will hope to the latest direst extremity."[30]

A number of Confederates thought Lee should exercise the greatest possible control of the war effort. A young artillerist observed in July 1864 that he wanted the general to direct all Confederate military operations. "In fact I should like to see him as King or Dictator," avowed this man. "He is one of the few great men who ever lived, who could be trusted." Rumors circulating in Richmond during late 1864 suggested that others agreed with this opinion. They told of an effort afoot, observed a government clerk, "to transfer some of the powers of the Executive to Gen. Lee . . . [I]t is believed many executive officers, some in high position, favor the scheme." A day later this diarist stated that "Nearly all desire to see Lee at the head of affairs."[31]

The Virginia legislature addressed a letter to President Davis on January 17, 1865, urging Lee's appointment "to command all the armies of the Confederate States," a move the legislators predicted would "operate powerfully to reanimate the spirits of the Armies, as well as of the people of the several States, and to inspire increased confidence in the final success of our cause." Lee's belated elevation to that post stimulated a brief surge in Confederate spirits. "Lee has taken command as Generalissimo," wrote a Virginia artillerist, "great things are expected from it, unity of aim, promptness, vigour." Another soldier thought that Lee's promotion "has inspired our country with more hope, courage, & confidence than it has had for a year or two."[32]

Lee himself displayed a firm Confederate nationalism conspicuously at odds with the widely held modern notion that he fought only to protect his native state. On Christmas Day 1861, he urged Mrs. Lee to dismiss the idea of ever returning to Arlington. The enemy's presence at the estate for several months had made it uninhabitable. The Lees could retain fond memories of the place, but now should look to the future, repent their transgressions against God, and anticipate a time when the "heavy punishment under which we labour may with justice be removed from us & the whole nation." Four days later he deplored the Confederate people's unawareness of what it would take to win independence. "We must make up our minds to fight our battles ourselves," he wrote. "Expect to receive aid from no one. Make every necessary sacrifice of comfort, money & labour to bring the war to a successful issue & then we will succeed. The cry is too much for help."

Just after the battle of Fredericksburg, he again expressed dismay at attitudes among the populace: "Oh if our people would only recognize it & cease from their vain self boasting & adulation, how strong would be my belief in final success & happiness to our country." In mid–1864 he closed a letter to Mary Custis Lee with a request that in her prayers she "never forget me or our suffering country."[33]

In speaking to his soldiers, Lee used language calculated to stir patriotism both in the ranks and, because his general orders often were published in newspapers, among people on the home front. During the harsh winter of 1864, for example, he apologized to his men for their reduced rations but added that "the history of the army has shown that the country can require no sacrifice too great for its patriotic devotion." Soldiers in the Army of Northern Virginia trod the same road down which their forefathers had "marched through suffering, privations, and blood, to independence." They would achieve as great a success if they continued "their high resolve to be free." As Lee doubtless hoped would be the case, the press and the public reacted to this general order. "Give the army subsistence," implored the Richmond *Enquirer*, "and the army will give the country peace." The people must equal the devotion of the soldiers, match them sacrifice for sacrifice, "in order that the army may perform the duty of defending the country." Debate over the system of impressment was idle: "Rations is the great question. Will the people supply General Lee with meat!" Diarist John B. Jones copied Lee's order in his journal and pronounced it "an eloquent and stirring appeal!"[34]

Both Lee and his soldiers came to understand the degree to which they sustained their nation's hopes for independence. Sometimes the burden oppressed them, as when Lee complained after Gettysburg about the "unreasonable expectations of the public" regarding the Army of Northern Virginia. More often, however, officers and men took pride in knowing they inspirited their fellow citizens. A trio of witnesses typified this attitude. "Lee's army is now the great hope of the South," wrote Edgeworth Bird to his wife in July 1863 after mentioning Confederate failures at Vicksburg and Port Hudson. "The army here thinks it can whip its weight in wild cats and has no mistrusts or apprehension." A member of the 9th Louisiana Infantry just back from a trip to Georgia in March 1864 confessed that he "never had the most distant idea of the honors that our army had gained till I visited Georgia; the mere name of being one of the Army of Northern Virginia is sufficient to pass one into the best circles of society down in Ga." Six months later, a captain in the 6th Georgia Infantry voiced a sentiment pervasive inside and outside the army: "The Army of Northern Virginia alone, as the last hope of the South, . . . will sooner or later by its own unaided power win the independence of the Confederacy."[35]

Because northern and southern newspapers made much of the odds Lee's army faced as 1864 took its frightful toll, some soldiers specifically urged those at home not to be intimidated by northern numbers or claims about Ulysses S. Grant's prowess. Lt. Col. Richard H. Dulany of the 7th Virginia Cavalry instructed his daughter just after Cold Harbor to "say to your Grandpa that Genl. Lee, having now successfully repulsed every effort of what the Yanks call the greatest living general and by far the mightiest army ever raised, he must now consider our cause stronger and our prospects brighter than ever." Another Virginia cavalryman employed far more colorful language in making the same point. Selecting an official day of fasting and prayer to give his mother "a scolding for being in bad spirits when there is no occasion for it whatever," James Keith implored her to think nothing of Lincoln's call for another million Union soldiers: "If he gets them God help the poor fools & let them take a last look at all they love if love they can for Lee is an insatiable monster & would gobble up a few more hundred thousand Yanks & lick his chops for more."[36]

Although far less frequently discussed by historians than the negative effect of desperate letters reaching soldiers from their families, men in the army employed various strategies to promote support for the Confederacy on the home front. Knowing that their morale generally remained higher than that of civilians, soldiers touted the army's confidence to family and friends while on furlough—a practice Brig. Gen. Clement A. Evans thought encouraged the spread of "the soldier's spirit of cheerfulness." They also wrote letters to local newspapers, many of which were reprinted by editors in other communities. Most often they corresponded with kinfolk, as Dulany and Keith did about northern numbers, affirming the army's determination and urging everyone behind the lines to be hopeful and supportive. "I fear that our people at home are becomeing too despondent [and] are whiped now," wrote a Georgia captain employing a widely used formula. "The old veterans of Lee's army isent whiped," he averred, "never has been, and I think [it] will be a long time before they are whiped . . . [L]et us be hopeful [and] as cheerful as possable under the circumstances; allways hope for the best [even] if the worst comes." In March 1864, Lt. Ted Barclay of the 4th Virginia chided his sister about gloomy attitudes behind the lines: "I am glad to see the tone of the people is becoming more courageous and more worthy of Southerners battling for freedom and all that men hold dear." She should "look at our noble army," he added, "voluntarily reenlisting for the war, none are found who shirk from their duty."[37]

Mass reenlistments ranked among the most dramatic and effective methods of sending a message from the Confederate army to the home front. In the spring of 1864, numerous units announced their reenlistment for the duration of the war. Some soldiers complained that officers manipulated the process to give the appearance of unified spirit, while others noted that Congress would find ways to keep them in the ranks whether they volunteered to stay or not.[38] Congress eventually did decree that men already in service would have to remain there, but most reenlistments in early 1864 seem to have been motivated by patriotism. Although congressional action rendered the reenlistments meaningless on one level, the willingness of men to volunteer further service had impressed many people behind the lines—none more than Jefferson Davis. In February 1864, the president gave public thanks: "Again you come to tender your service for the public defense—a free offering, which only such patriotism as yours could make—a triumph worthy of you and of the cause to which you are devoted . . . Already the pulse of the whole people beats in unison with yours . . . Even the murmurs of the weak and timid, who shrink from the trials which make stronger and firmer your noble natures, are shamed into silence by the spectacle which you present." Newspapers joined the president in lauding the soldiers, as when the Richmond *Enquirer* observed that "the prompt and patriotic action of the army in re-enlisting for the war" had "infused new life and spirit into the people." In winning a victory "over self" the soldiers had shown the people that "they, too, have a victory to win—a victory over unrighteous mammon, a victory for the country."[39]

Civilians across the Confederacy characterized the reenlistments as uplifting manifestations of loyalty to the Confederacy. Testimony from three women in Alabama, Virginia, and South Carolina suggests the tenor of many comments. From Mobile, Kate Cumming reported hearing that all of James Longstreet's First Corps "has re-enlisted for the war, no matter how long it may last. Our whole army has done the same." Virginian Georgiana Gholson Walker praised Davis's official statement to the troops as a "noble, grand address . . . full of patriotism & of gratitude to & pride in the Sons of the South!" The president's "whole soul seems to be melted by this renewed proof of the loyalty of his people," Walker wrote happily. "What a contrast to the bribes & threats & false pretences of our enemy!" Emma Holmes's diary displayed comparable enthusiasm. "The whole army is animated with the brightest & most determined spirit," recorded the South Carolinian, "and almost everywhere the soldiers are re-enlisting unanimously, by companies, regiments or brigades for *the war,* (& one body added) even if it lasts 40 years."[40]

A second round of unit reenlistments followed the failure of the Hampton Roads peace conference in February 1865. Regiments, battalions, and some brigades drafted resolutions for distribution to politicians and newspapers. Hoping to bolster civilian morale at a time when desertions had increased (dramatically in some units), the soldiers emphatically stated that differences between the North and South defied reconciliation, that the army retained morale comparable to that of their revolutionary forefathers, and that with full support from civilians and the government, Lee and his army would win independence on the battlefield. Explaining the purpose of the resolutions to his sister, Capt. Charles Fenton James of the 8th Virginia Infantry wrote that "after four years of bloody war—of hardships and privations, the veteran soldiers of the invincible army of Northern Virginia, are speaking to the country."[41] Lee expressed gratification "with the meetings which had been held and the resolutions adopted in some Regts. and Brigades" in a letter published in the newspapers.[42]

The prestige and symbolic importance of Lee and his army were such that few Confederates contemplated serious resistance after Appomattox. Never mind that Lee surrendered only a fraction of the southern soldiers under arms in April 1865. The death of the Army of Northern Virginia removed the Confederate people's cherished rallying point and effectively marked the demise of their nation. Across the Confederacy, soldiers and civilians reacted with dismay. "My last hope died within me when Genl Lee surrendered," a major serving in the Trans-Mississippi admitted to his father in May 1865. Word of Lee's surrender reached Virginian Sarah Strickler Fife on April 11, prompting an anguished diary entry: "I cannot keep off the terrible feeling that I am standing at the death bed of the dearest thing on earth to me." A young Floridian received the blow in similar fashion. "General Lee has surrendered the Army of Northern Virginia," she wrote. "Oh, I wish we were all dead! It is as if the very earth had crumbled beneath our feet."[43]

Within the army that served as such a symbol of Confederate nationalism, slaveholding officers who had reached maturity during the 1850s may have provided the emotional core. This is a crucial group because the median age of Lee's field-grade officers (majors, lieutenant colonels, and colonels) was thirty-one at the time of appointment. Company-grade officers (second lieutenants, lieutenants, and captains) almost certainly were even younger. No one has examined Confederate nationalism from a generational perspective,[44] but the letters and diaries of men in their early twenties to early thirties reveal similarities of outlook that predisposed many of them to be faithful Confederates. Although no generalizations apply to all members of any large group, several tentative observations seem to fit a majority of these men. Reared among the sectional controversies of the late 1840s and 1850s, they harbored few if any doubts about the institution of slavery, attributed base motives to northerners in general and Republicans in particular, often spoke of a distinct cultural identity for the South, and supported secession and united southern action when the crisis broke in the winter of 1860–61. Once fighting began, they advanced through the army's command to lead companies, regiments, brigades, and divisions of infantry and cavalry and batteries and battalions of artillery. Many compiled records of conspicuous bravery and accomplishment, won renown, and wielded considerable influence over their men.[45] Steadfastly devoted to the Confederacy, they remained outspoken advocates of continued sacrifice until the very last days of the conflict.

Many of these young men manifested a sense of southern nationalism before they became Confederates.[46] Political friction related to slavery in the 1850s often prompted categorical defenses of slavery and insistence that compromise held no long-term promise for the South. A pair of reactions to the presidential canvass of 1856 touched on common themes. From West Point, cadet Stephen Dodson Ramseur of North Carolina applauded James Buchanan's victory but pronounced it only a temporary check on antislavery forces in the North. "Any man of the smallest observation can plainly see, that the Union of the States cannot exist harmoniously," stated Ramseur. Northerners had supported Republican John C. Frémont—"a renegade, a cheat and a *liar*"—solely because he opposed slavery, "the very source of our existence, the *greatest blessing* for both master & slave, that could have been bestowed upon us." Arguing that the sections differed so markedly in manners and education as to be two different countries, Ramseur believed that the South should "establish armories, collect stores & provide for the most desperate of all calamities—civil war." A Georgian also emphasized the divided nature of the vote in 1856 and anticipated a showdown with the North. "The next issue will doubtless be purely sectional in character," wrote Charles C. Jones, Jr. "The prospect is fearful, but everything indicates such a future condition of affairs. And when it does come, we of the South must and will be prepared to meet it bravely and without concession."[47]

More than 900 field officers in Lee's army—roughly half of all who served—graduated from colleges and universities. Of those, 44 percent attended institutions in Virginia. Students on Virginia's campuses during the 1850s thus deserve notice, and ample evidence suggests that many of them defended slavery ostentatiously, portrayed the North as a predatory menace, and exhibited a pronounced allegiance to the South. In January 1851, for example, in the wake of the Compromise of 1850, 115 members of the Southern Rights Association at the University of Virginia signed an address calculated to promote a collective southern identity. After listing basic differences between the sections, which included free versus slave labor and a manufacturing versus an agricultural economy, these students implored counterparts throughout the South "to resist, 'to the last extremity and at every hazard,' the wrongs and aggressions of the North." The signatories affirmed that all political compromises with the North had failed. Southern rights and liberties had been attacked and could "only be preserved by firm, decisive and united action, which we maintain can best be attained by directing the attention of the young men of the South to the wrongs and insults which have been heaped upon them, and awakening in their breasts a spirit of determined, resolute resistance."[48]

Lectures and student publications similarly conjured images of the South and its social fabric at risk from a rapacious abolitionist North. In his "Medal Speech" at Emory & Henry College in June 1855, twenty-four-year-old John L. Buchanan blasted the "fanatical spirit of the North" that had "engaged in an unholy crusade upon Southern rights." Harriet Beecher Stowe's *Uncle Tom's Cabin* had slandered slaveholders and given ammunition to foreigners who hated slavery and the South. If the "remorseless spirit of Northern aggression" continued to advance, predicted Buchanan, Americans would witness "a fiery storm-cloud of desolation, whose lightnings will shiver this Union into atoms and whose thunders will peal the funeral dirge of the last republic." Five years after publication of Mrs. Stowe's novel, students at Hampton Academy heard another speaker (an 1852 graduate of the school) thunder against "systematic falsehood, arrayed in the seductive shape of a vicious novel." Having been "taught from youth to believe, and being better assured of it from the studies of our manhood, that the institution of slavery is divine in its origin," the students in the audience should strive to create a southern literature to combat lies disseminated by writers such as Stowe. That might not be sufficient, the speaker added darkly, and the time could come when the Constitution no longer protected southern interests. From that moment, he would "view it simply as a broken contract, not binding on the parties."[49]

Belief in southern exceptionalism and an explicit threat of disunion stand out in two last pieces of late antebellum evidence from Virginia schools. In 1859, a monthly magazine published by students at Hampden Sidney College urged southern youth not to attend northern schools because they might imbibe ideas inimical to their slave-based society. The South was "unalterably identified with slave institutions, slave property and slave labor . . . The people of the South believe that the prosperity and existence of our Union depend upon the maintenance of that institution—the people of the North believe that the prosperity and existence of the Union depend upon its destruction." Education in the North for southerners "would not only unfit them for their native institutions, but at the same time implant in them a deadly hostility to the institution which nothing but its destruction could appease." A student at Emory & Henry similarly sketched two different cultures in an 1854 article—an abolitionist North welcoming "hordes of foreigners" and a stable slaveholding South. The North should "remember that upon the *security of Southern rights depends the perpetuity of this Union*," warned this young man, "and that a continued war upon these rights may change our love to hate—our forbearance to a thirst for the aggressors' blow and plunge our devoted country into all the horrors of civil war."[50]

Not surprisingly, the secession crisis found many of these men willing to break with the North and join a southern republic. Their identification with the South seamlessly transmuted into a strong Confederate identity. Edward Porter Alexander, a twenty-five-year-old Georgian and lieutenant of engineers in the United States Army, followed events during 1860 from Fort Steilacoom in Washington Territory. Generally considered among the most dispassionate of Confederates because of his evenhanded postwar memoirs, Alexander evinced strong emotional ties to the South in 1860. Speculation that Lincoln probably won the presidential canvass (definitive word would not reach the West Coast for many days) prompted an unequivocal response from Alexander on November 11. "We suppose from the latest news we have that Lincoln is elected, and if so I *hope* and *expect* to be called in to help secede," he wrote one of his sisters. Once inaugurated, Lincoln would control the military and financial power of the country, making it "too late to oppose him." In the event of a Republican victory, Alexander saw but one path for himself and the slaveholding South: "I believe the interests of humanity, civilization, and self-preservation call on the South to secede, and I'll go my arm, leg, or death on it." From Texas, Thomas Jewett Goree, who would serve on James Longstreet's staff during the Civil War, similarly believed Lincoln's election to be intolerable. A former booster of Unionist Sam Houston, the twenty-five-year-old Goree called for "immediate secession" in December 1860. When the Texas state convention met in January 1861, Goree hoped his state would "promptly secede from a Union which is no longer worth preserving."[51]

The actions of individuals from the Upper South are especially instructive. They might have been expected to waffle until the firing on Fort Sumter and Lincoln's call for 75,000 volunteers; however, many took action long before their states aligned themselves with the Confederacy. Illustrative of this group were William Dorsey Pender and Stephen Dodson Ramseur, officers in the United States army in 1860 but destined to become Confederate major generals, who lost patience with their native North Carolina's slow reaction to Lincoln's election. Pender resigned in March and Ramseur in early April, and both immediately offered their services to the Confederacy. When Pender's wife, Fanny, questioned his decision, he replied that he had "acted for the best . . . I shall never regret resigning, whatever may turn up." On April 3, Pender sent her a Confederate flag. "That is our Flag," he told Fanny sternly, "for it is yours as much as mine and by it you must stick." Weeks passed and Pender chafed at North Carolina's vacillation. "I am disgusted with North Carolina," he wrote on May 4. If the legislature did not take action soon, "N.C. is a doomed state—either to subjection or eternal disgrace."[52]

Among the few non-Virginia cadets at the Virginia Military Institute, nineteen-year-old North Carolinian Henry King Burgwyn, Jr., also fretted over the state's lack of action. In January 1861, he condemned the "treachery" of Winfield Scott in recommending the use of coercion against the seceded states. Burgwyn, who would become a Confederate colonel at age twenty and die in action at Gettysburg, believed the cotton states should seize all federal forts within their borders before United States garrisons could be increased. Although North Carolina's secession lay more than four months in the future, he hoped "that our old state may be waked into something like a decided course of conduct." A postscript asked, "Is there any prospect of Gov. Ellis' taking forts Macon & Johnston?" Burgwyn already had made it plain that he would fight to defend southern rights if necessary. The previous December, he had seen no chance for "any pacific settlement of the questions now at issue between the North & South" and had asked that his father procure for him "a situation in the N.C. Volunteers." Put off by the absence of any true concessions on the part of Republican politicians, Burgwyn stated: "My feelings would cause me to think that a settlement can not be made until some of our grievances have been settled by the sword. Whatever happens I am ready."[53]

During the early months of 1861, many young Virginians similarly criticized the Old Dominion's reluctance to embrace secession. Burgwyn's fellow cadets at VMI, virtually all of whom would serve in the Army of Northern Virginia, repeatedly raised secession flags and clashed with local unionists. A debate on George Washington's birthday among students in a literary society at Washington College yielded a 43–8 majority for secession. At about the same time, a student at the University of Virginia wrote his mother from Charlottesville that "the feeling amongst the students here is now almost, though not quite, unanimous in favor of immediate secession." During a mock election in November 1860, students in Charlottesville had cast a majority for John Bell and the moderate Constitutional Union Party, but Lincoln's election and South Carolina's secession "had the effect of crystalizing among them what had previously been a more or less fluctuating sentiment in support of the general theory of secession."[54]

A pair of young Virginians who subsequently became artillerists in Lee's army voiced opinions typical of those who placed southern interests above the Union. Twenty-two-year-old John Hampden Chamberlayne called for Virginia's secession immediately after Lincoln won the presidency. Three months later, after thanking God "for the fixed fact of a Southern Confederacy," Chamberlayne rendered a harsh judgment about his home state's course of action: "If Virginia has the baseness to barter her self respect for the position of tail end of the northern power, I at least and the whole family whom I represent will leave Virginia forever, and I know many who will do the same." William Ransom Johnson Pegram, a student at the University of Virginia in 1860–61 who would win fame commanding an artillery battalion, spoke no less firmly about the crisis. Worried about the South's slave-based society, Pegram reflected on the results of the election of 1860: "We have a President, opposed to us in every way, and a vice-President, who is to preside over that august body, the Senate of the United States, a half-negro; and the Germans for our *masters.*" Pegram later disapproved of the Crittenden Compromise as "no improvement whatever on the Constitution." While he did not relish the prospect of "the greatest of all evils, '*a civil war,*'" Pegram left no doubt that his attachment to the South and its peculiar institution would overshadow any loyalty to the Union.[55]

Once in the Confederate army, virtually all of these young officers exhibited a tenacious patriotism. They insisted on full commitment to the Confederacy, retained their sense of duty even after the war had turned overwhelmingly in favor of Union arms, and frequently gave their lives attempting to rally soldiers in seemingly hopeless situations. Alexander Swift "Sandie" Pendleton, who would serve as the chief staff officer in the Second Corps for much of the war, articulated a typically unsparing standard of duty when he learned of the surrender of the Confederate garrison at Fort Donelson in February 1862. "I am thoroughly disgusted, not disheartened," he wrote. "What could have possessed our generals at Fort Donelson? Are they demented? Or do they not know that our struggle has to be carried on desperately, and with the determination to die rather than be conquered." The Confederate soldiers who surrendered at Fort Donelson were "thinking too much of a whole skin, and too little of their country and the future. What difference does a few hours more or less here of life make in comparison with the future destiny of the people?"[56]

Many of these men also exhibited a ferocious antipathy toward the enemy reminiscent of their implacable hatred of abolitionists before the war. The imagined repugnance of life under Union rule helped fire Confederate nationalism. Anyone cherishing the romantic notion of a brothers' war marked by tender scenes of fraternization between Union and Confederate soldiers should heed the words of young officers such as Porter Alexander. When an older comrade remarked that Confederates did not hate Yankees as individuals and always treated northern prisoners well, Alexander quickly responded: "I always feel like kicking their prisoners all around. [I]t is my greatest comfort to know that I have killed some of them with my own hands, I have shot them with muskets and artillery and have seen them fall and afterwards went there and found them dead. [I]f they should kill me today and I had but time for one thought before I died," he concluded, "it would be that my account with them was more than even."[57]

Throughout the war, young officers urged fellow Confederates to treat setbacks as no more than temporary obstacles on the path to independence. Two letters from the Shenandoah Valley in October 1864 illustrate this phenomenon. Dodson Ramseur pressed his wife, Ellen, to see that southern defeats at Winchester and Fisher's Hill and the probability of Lincoln's re-election were not cause for disillusionment. "Our disaster in the Valley—with Hood's at Atlanta makes me think the war party will triumph at the North," he admitted, "But tho' peace may be a long way off, I feel sure that Justice & Right will finally triumph." Rather than give in to despair, Ellen should prepare for even greater privations and hardships with the thought that "Surely all true Southrons would prefer *anything* to *submission*." Shortly after Ramseur wrote, a twenty-five-year-old staff officer in the 4th Virginia Cavalry railed against "all submissionists & reconstructionists [and] all those who sigh for peace without first an aspiration for independence." Winter would afford an opportunity to gather strength for another campaign in the spring of 1865, when "we shall be once more ready to prove to them that however weary we may be of war the feeling is not of the kind to make us abate one jot or title of our just demands & that southern blood is still ready to flow in defense of southern rights."[58]

Men such as Walter H. Taylor and Willy Pegram held a dogged expectation of Confederate success until the very end, doing their best to inspirit those who wavered. Probably the staff officer closest to Lee throughout the war, Taylor welcomed news of the failed Confederate peace mission in February 1865. "I hope all the croakers are satisfied and will hereafter keep silent," wrote the twenty-six-year-old Virginian to his fiancée. "Our people now know what they have to expect & unless we are a craven hearted spiritless people, the result will surely prove beneficial & cause every man & woman to be doubly determined to fight to the last." The disheartened tone of a letter from his sister Mary in March 1865 prompted Pegram to describe the Army of Northern Virginia as "cheerful and hopeful." Surrounded in Richmond by what he termed "croakers and cowards," Mary should not credit rumors "conceived in their craven hearts, and spread by every idle tongue." Only if she resisted defeatist gossip could she hope to "look coolly or dispassionately" on prospects for Confederate victory. Overall, Pegram believed the military situation was "growing brighter every day."[59]

Pegram's spirit seems to have influenced the soldiers of his battalion, as evidenced by a letter penned during the retreat to Appomattox. "How my heart yearns to the men who have followed for four years the shining saber of my peerless Colonel," wrote William Gordon McCabe, the battalion's ordnance officer. "Hungry, wet, with blistered feet, without sleep, they have stood by their guns & fought with a desperation, a superb courage that I never dreamed of . . . They will go with Genl. Lee as long as the Battle-Cross floats on the field."[60]

Disagreement with government policies did little to diminish feelings of Confederate nationalism among these younger officers—a fact underscored by their reaction to the debate over arming slaves. As firm proslavery men, most of them would have preferred that the institution survive the war unaltered. Walter Taylor worked for the person most responsible for the government's decision to attempt to enroll black soldiers, a situation that might have been awkward at times but did not lessen Taylor's commitment to the Confederacy. "What do you think of the question of negro soldiers now?" he asked his fiancee in mid-February 1865. "It makes me sad . . . to reflect that the time honoured institution will be no more, that the whole social organization of the South is to be revolutionized," he observed: "But I suppose it is all right and we will have to be reconciled." John Hampden Chamberlayne's proslavery zeal fully matched Taylor's, yet he not only accepted the idea of black soldiers but also favored compelling them to serve. "How are negro enlistments getting on?" he inquired three days before Richmond fell. "They seem to me very slow, conscription will be necessary. And even then the number will not be great, I fear."[61]

Perhaps the greatest indication of Confederate nationalism among young officers lay in their recklessly exposing themselves in combat to help achieve independence. Of those quoted here, Dorsey Pender and Harry Burgwyn had died of wounds long before the war turned decisively toward the North. Three others, however, continued to display conspicuously dangerous personal leadership in action at a stage of the conflict when many of their fellow citizens believed northern victory to be certain. Three months shy of his twenty-fourth birthday, Willy Pegram was shot from his saddle at Five Forks on April 1, 1865, as he urged his gunners to aim their fire low at masses of advancing Federals. The previous fall, on September 22, 1864, "Sandie" Pendleton, also twenty-three years old, had been mortally wounded while attempting to rally Confederates along the Valley Turnpike following the rout at Fisher's Hill. Dodson Ramseur, three months past his twenty-seventh birthday and a division commander, received a mortal wound at Cedar Creek on October 19, 1864, after rallying fragments of several units for more than hour in the face of an overpowering Federal assault. Ramseur repeatedly had proved his capacity to lead, remarked Army of the Valley commander Jubal A. Early shortly after the battle, "but never did those qualities shine more conspicuously than on the afternoon of the 19th." A member of Ramseur's staff present at the deathbed wrote on October 20 that the general "died as became a Confederate soldier and a firm believer."[62]

Ramseur's staff officer touched an important point in stating that his superior had died as a *Confederate* soldier. Ramseur thought of himself as a soldier for the Confederate *nation,* and that was a major element in how untold other young officers, as well as the men they led and inspired, thought of themselves. Superior performances of units commanded by many of these men suggest that the soldiers followed their example on the battlefield. Early's observation about Ramseur's leadership at Cedar Creek addressed the way in which determination to sacrifice for the Confederacy seemingly radiated outward from highly motivated officers to the men they commanded. Ramseur's brigade was among those with a high proportion of reenlistments in the winter of 1864, and a captain in the 2nd North Carolina Infantry wrote in 1864 that Ramseur was "universally beloved by every man in his brigade. No braver or better man lives than he is. He takes good care of his soldiers . . . fights hard and is very successful. His men like to fight under him." Another captain lamented the youthful North Carolinian's death because he ranked among "the best fighters we had."[63]

Conclusions about the overall impact of young slaveholding officers such as Ramseur must remain tentative. These men almost certainly ranked among the staunchest Confederate nationalists—and thus expose the shallowness of arguments that depict most slaveholders as selfish and only superficially identified with the Confederacy. By Lee's own testimony, as well as that of men such as the officers who praised Ramseur and Willy Pegram, their contributions to the success of the Army of Northern Virginia cannot be gainsaid. In that way, they surely strengthened feelings of national community.[64] They also did their best through letters and by personal example in combat to inspire others inside and outside the military. But how did the rank and file view them? Did the young officers infuse yeomen soldiers with some of their own ardor, or were they perceived as slaveholding elitists whose Confederate enthusiasm had little relevance to common folk? And what of the officers' impact on civilians? Did their physical bravery in action and exhortations in letters stiffen the resolve of family and friends, or was the gulf between the men in the army and those behind the lines too wide to bridge?[65] Answers to these questions must await further study.

Contrary to what many modern scholars suggest, it can be stated with a fair degree of certainty that thousands of soldiers in the Army of Northern Virginia developed strong feelings of Confederate nationalism that helped drive them toward military success and fame. Their achievements and reputation in turn nourished patriotism and resolve among civilians. But could the soldiers' efforts have been put to even better advantage by the South's political and military leadership? The relationship between military strategy and Confederate nationalism and popular will was central to the southern war effort.

President-elect Jefferson Davis addresses a crowd outside the Exchange Hotel in Montgomery, Alabama, on February 16, 1861. Speaking two days before his inauguration as Confederate president, Davis articulated a strong sense of national feeling: "For now we are brethren, not in name, merely, but in fact—men of one flesh, one bone, one interest, one purpose, and of identity of domestic institutions." (*Frank Leslie's Illustrated Newspaper,* March 16, 1861)

The Confederacy's attempt to construct a nation included patriotic music. "God Save the South," a work composed by Maryland poet and dramatist George H. Miles, was among the more successful efforts to produce a national anthem. This illustrated cover appeared on one of the nine Confederate editions of Miles's piece. (Library of Congress)

Jefferson Davis proclaimed days of fasting and prayer that gave many Confederates a sense of sacrificing for national purpose. The northern press took a more cynical view of these proclamations, as shown by this cartoon of emaciated Confederates reading a broadside while a horned Davis stands off to the side. (Collection of the author)

The plight of refugees, as depicted in this wartime sketch of people encamped in woods near Vicksburg, Mississippi, prompted many Confederate soldiers and civilians to renew their determination to defeat the North. (*Illustrated London News,* August 29, 1863)

On November 22, 1862, Robert E. Lee commented about refugees from Fredericksburg who had moved west when the Union army prepared to occupy the city. "It has been very cold & still is," he wrote Mrs. Lee: "I was moving out the women & children all last night & today. It was a pitious sight." In David English Henderson's 1865 painting, some of these refugees gather around a fire. (Gettysburg National Military Park)

Few photographs offer a more poignant view of the war's impact on civilians than this study of a family, its possessions lashed to a single wagon, preparing to join the ranks of thousands of other refugees across the Confederacy. (Library of Congress)

This crude wartime engraving presented three generations of Confederates inspired by the example of their nation's soldiers marching to fight the battle of Chickamauga. The caption reads: "Yes, my children; there they come, our country's deliverers. We are now safe from the tyrant." (Confederate Imprints Collection, University of Georgia, Athens)

STIRRING APPEAL.

Willingness to enroll black soldiers if necessary to achieve Confederate independence highlighted the sense of collective national loyalty that many white southerners had developed by 1864–65. *Harper's Weekly* offered this satirical comment on the Confederate debate over arming black men. "Here! you mean, inferior, degraded Chattel, jest kitch holt of one of them 'ere muskits, and *conquer my freedom for me!*" states the "Chivalric Southerner." The "Chattel" responds: "Well, dunno, Massa; guess you'd better not be free: you know, Massa, *slave folks is deal happier than free folks.*" (*Harper's Weekly,* December 10, 1864)

Military victories proved crucial to the nourishment of national sentiment in the Confederacy. In this engraving, residents of Richmond cheer a one-hundred-gun salute marking the success at First Manassas. (Paul F. Mottelay and T. Campbell Copeland, eds., *The Soldier in Our Civil War: Columbian Memorial Edition. A Pictorial History of the Conflict, 1861–1865,* 2 vols. New York: Stanley Bradley Publishing Co., 1893, 1:109)

Robert E. Lee in martial dress, a full-length view probably taken in early 1863. The Army of Northern Virginia supplied virtually all of the South's major victories, and Confederates responded by looking to Lee and his army as their most important national rallying point. (Francis Trevelyan Miller, ed., *The Photographic History of the Civil War,* 10 vols. New York: Review of Reviews, 1911, 2:235)

Stephen Dodson Ramseur, a North Carolinian who manifested the strong nationalistic feeling common among young slaveholding officers in Lee's army, was deeply antagonistic toward the North and believed the Confederate people should make any sacrifice to gain independence. In January 1864, as Lee's army suffered through a harsh winter of short rations, Ramseur assured his brother-in-law that he and his brigade were *"in for the war without* condition . . . we intend to *fight* the *thing out*—. . . [*and*] *we won't be whipped* as long as anybody is left to fight." (Collection of the author)

The rank and file of the Army of Northern Virginia made possible the victories that sustained national morale in the Confederacy. No photograph taken in the field better illustrates the appearance of veteran Confederate troops than this view of three of Lee's soldiers captured at Gettysburg. "Language is inadequate to convey an idea of the supreme confidence this army reposes in its great and good leader," wrote one of Lee's men. (Francis Trevelyan Miller, ed., *The Photographic History of the Civil War,* 10 vols. New York: Review of Reviews, 1911, 1:103)

General Joseph Eggleston Johnston, whose penchant for defensive strategy prompted many Confederates to question his military leadership. Among the harshest critics was southern ordnance chief Josiah Gorgas, who commented in May 1864 about Johnston's retreat toward Atlanta: "It is surmised that he will reach Macon in a few days at the rate he is retreating. I trust the country will sooner or later find out what sort of a General he is. I don't think he will suit the emergency." (Francis Trevelyan Miller, ed., *The Photographic History of the Civil War,* 10 vols. New York: Review of Reviews, 1911, 10:241)

A group of Lee's soldiers at Sayler's Creek, Virginia, April 6, 1865, hold their muskets and battle flag in positions indicating capitulation to Federal troops. Three days later Lee surrendered the remainder of his army, extinguishing serious hopes for founding a Confederate nation. (Robert Underwood Johnson and Clarence Clough Buel, eds., *Battles and Leaders of the Civil War,* 4 vols. New York: Century, 1887–88, 4:721)

3

MILITARY STRATEGY

"The Southern populace clamoured for bloody battles"

The style and substance of Confederate military strategy sprang directly from the expectations of the southern people. In a relationship typical of a democracy at war, citizens demanded of their leaders a strategy that would affirm nationalistic strivings and thus nourish popular will. Ironically, the strategy best calculated to meet these ends also extracted a hideous price in battlefield casualties that compromised the southern war effort. The contest came down to one great question: Would the Confederacy's strategy secure nationhood before it depleted precious human and material resources to a point guaranteeing northern triumph? The key to success lay in winning clear-cut victories on the battlefield that would depress Union morale as they bolstered Confederate will, while at the same time convincing Britain and France that recognition—or even intervention—would serve their national interests. Robert E. Lee, his officer corps, and the soldiers they commanded supplied many, but in the end not enough, such victories.

Confronted with a daunting range of military challenges, Jefferson Davis chose to pursue what many historians have labeled an "offensive-defensive" strategy. This consisted of fielding large national armies, placing them in an overarching defensive posture to protect as much territory as possible, and launching offensive movements against northern armies when circumstances promised success. Robert E. Lee, who functioned as Davis's most important military adviser and only successful field commander, emphasized the "offensive" in offensive-defensive, seeking always to find a way to gain and hold the strategic and tactical initiative. Within a framework largely shaped by Davis in the Western Theater and Lee in the Eastern Theater, Confederate arms fought numerous bloody battles, raised civilian hopes for victory, stretched northern will to the limit on more than one occasion, and ultimately failed to achieve independence.[1]

That failure does not mean Confederate strategy was deeply flawed.[2] Indeed, three times southern military operations seriously threatened northern civilian morale: first in the late summer of 1862, when armies under Lee and Braxton Bragg moved into the Border States of Maryland and Kentucky, and Great Britain edged toward some type of intervention; again in the spring of 1863, after Lee had turned back successive northern advances into Virginia, and Union operations against Vicksburg had yielded nothing; and finally in the summer of 1864, when the North grimly tallied the losses of the Overland campaign, and the armies of U. S. Grant and William Tecumseh Sherman bogged down outside Richmond and Atlanta.[3] Potential for further Confederate success in the first two instances lay with Lee, who sought through movements into Maryland in September 1862 and into Pennsylvania the following June to continue the momentum generated in pairs of victories at the Seven Days and Second Manassas and later at Fredericksburg and Chancellorsville. Another victory in either instance might have changed significantly the strategic picture. Other might-have-beens—if a siege comparable to that at Petersburg had stymied Sherman outside Atlanta until after the elections of 1864, for example— yield endless speculative permutations, but the point is that the strategy implemented by Davis and his generals made sense and more than once brought their cause close to victory.

Defeat predictably opened the door to generations of second-guessing about Confederate strategy. During the war, there had been sharp debates over the strategic allocation of troops—most notably in the spring and summer of 1863 regarding Lee's army in Virginia and the armies defending the Mississippi River and the Chattanooga-Atlanta heartland. Confederates also had argued the virtues of a defensive versus an offensive overall strategy, as well as the relative merits of dispersing forces throughout the country or gathering them in a few large armies that could be shifted to meet the strongest Union threats.[4] Once the war ended, critics stepped forward with a range of opinions about how the Confederacy could have put its resources to better use. Many of the arguments worked backward from Appomattox. The Confederacy lost. Assuming it had begun the conflict with at least some chance of victory, it must have relied on a flawed strategy. If that were the case, what strategic alternative should Confederates have chosen?

An initial round of analysis, most of which focused on Jefferson

Davis, emanated from former Confederate officers. Typical of those who faulted the president's strategy were P. G. T. Beauregard and Joseph E. Johnston, both of whom had feuded with Davis for much of the war and hoped to even old scores. The Confederacy would have won, contended Beauregard, if not for Davis's "timid policy" that left manpower scattered "in inferior relative strength at all parts of the compass." Beauregard had recommended massing manpower for decisive offensives but lost out to Davis's "passive mode of warfare." Even Lee, believed Beauregard, had been "perhaps a little too cautious in civil as well as Mil[i]t[ar]y matters." Johnston, in contrast, castigated Davis for trying to force him to be more aggressive during the Atlanta campaign. Had Davis permitted him to continue his conservative defensive strategy against Sherman, implied Johnston, Atlanta would have been saved. That in turn could have ensured Confederate independence: "If Sherman had been foiled, . . . [it] would have strengthened the peace party [in the North] greatly; so much, perhaps, as to have enabled it to carry the presidential election, which would have brought the war to an immediate close."[5]

Other former Confederates blamed Lee more than Davis, insisting that in the critical summer of 1863 he denied men to western Confederate armies that, if reinforced, might have saved Vicksburg and opened the way toward recovering parts of Middle Tennessee. James Longstreet had been one of a number of Confederates supporting a strategic shift of men from the Army of Northern Virginia to the West in 1863, and after the war he stood out among writers criticizing Lee's opposition to their plan. "I proposed to send a force through East Tennessee to join [Braxton] Bragg and also to have [Joseph E.] Johnston sent to join him," wrote Longstreet, "thus concentrating a large force to move against [William S.] Rosecrans, crush out his army, and march against Cincinnati. That, I thought, was the only way we had to relieve Vicksburg." Longstreet claimed that "General Lee admitted the force of my proposition, but finally stated that he preferred to organize a campaign into Maryland and Pennsylvania . . . After discussing the matter with him for several days, I found his mind made up not to allow any of his troops to go west." Lee went north, suffered a bloody repulse at Gettysburg, and retreated. "One mistake of the Confederacy was in pitting force against force," concluded Longstreet with respect to Lee's aggressive actions in Pennsylvania. "The only hope we had was to outgeneral the Federals . . . Our purpose should have been to impair the *morale* of the Federal army and shake Northern confidence in the Federal leaders."[6]

Two arguments have figured prominently in recent critiques of Confederate strategy. The more common of the pair alleges that Confederates too often took the strategic and tactical offensive. Burdened with the need to neutralize northern numbers, contend many historians, the South should have hewed to the defensive as often as possible. That type of warfare conserved manpower, and mid-nineteenth-century military developments—especially the widespread use of rifle muskets, which had a much longer range than smoothbores, and increasing reliance on field fortifications—added immeasurably to a defender's advantage over an attacker. Battlefield victories meant little in isolation; the crucial factor lay in keeping a Confederate military presence in the field to rally white southerners and vex their northern counterparts. Confederates therefore should have adopted a Fabian approach, trading territory for time, dragging the war out, and exhausting the North's national will.

An important corollary to the "too much offense" theory—a corollary that has overshadowed the broader theory—is that, of all Confederate commanders, Lee erred on the side of audacity most often, depleting the magnificent Army of Northern Virginia and thereby opening the way for Union victory. Even Lee's most strident critics concede that he won famous battles and earned a towering reputation, but they insist that his triumphs proved fleeting when measured against their dangerous diminution of southern white manpower. Confederate leaders need have looked no further than the American Revolution for proof that a weaker power, which claimed few victories and often retreated rather than confronting superior British forces, could achieve independence by wearing down the enemy's will.

The second common argument takes the Confederacy's leadership to task for not adopting a wide-scale guerrilla resistance from the beginning. Undoubtedly influenced by the American experience in Vietnam, historians articulating this notion envision small groups of Confederates striking at the enemy's extended lines of communication as increasingly frustrated Federals sought to bring rebel soldiers to battle in the vast southern hinterlands. Like those who extol the potential of a more rigorous defensive strategy, proponents of the guerrilla option muster a number of supporting points: Confederate manpower within this context would have lasted almost indefinitely; the northern public never would have countenanced the long-term commitment required to suppress dedicated guerrillas; the South was large enough to give up control of huge chunks of territory without materially damaging its cause; Confederate cavalry and irregular units in the Western Theater demonstrated the potential of such a strategy by halting Union advances after the fall of Corinth in the summer of 1862; and the Revolutionary War demonstrated how a guerrilla war for national liberation could succeed.

No one has offered a more powerful brief against aggressive warfare than Grady McWhiney and Perry D. Jamieson, who maintained that "the Confederates bled themselves nearly to death in the first three years of the war by making costly attacks more often than did the Federals." Despite heavy losses, southern leaders remained devoted to attacks because of their cultural background: "The Confederates favored offensive warfare because the Celtic charge was an integral part of their heritage." Confederates embraced the strategic as well as the tactical offensive, as evidenced by the fact that from the "war's outset southern sentiment overwhelmingly favored an invasion of the North." Quoting a colonel who remarked that outnumbered Confederates had "to take great risks" and use "activity, audacity, aggressiveness, and skill" to counter the North's numbers, McWhiney and Jamieson concluded, "Unfortunately for the Confederates, their willingness 'to take great risks' brought them no decisive victories and unbearable losses." Although few historians accepted the Celtic dimension of McWhiney and

Jamieson's thesis, their critique of offensive strategy and tactics reflected a broad strain in the literature.[7]

Robert E. Lee stands at the center of scholarship critical of Confederate offensive strategy and tactics.[8] McWhiney and Jamieson observed that he "liked the tactical offensive and assumed it whenever he could." Lee manifested his finest generalship when fighting on the defensive, they added, but adopted that mode "only after attrition had deprived him of the power to attack." Although his soldiers inflicted horrendous casualties on Grant's army during the Overland campaign in 1864, the Confederate commander had embarked on "defensive warfare too late; Lee started the campaign with too few men, and he could not replace his losses as could Grant." Thomas L. Connelly previously had criticized Lee for piling up 50,000 Confederate casualties during his first three months in command. In the course of Lee's tenure as its chief, stated Connelly, the Army of Northern Virginia "was bled to death by . . . [his] offensive tactics." Lee's most recent biographer also subscribed to this view. "From hindsight it is easy to see that Lee learned at least one negative lesson from the Mexican War," wrote Emory M. Thomas, "a precept he would have been wise to forget." Observing Winfield Scott's successful assaults against more numerous but poorly armed defenders during the war with Mexico, Lee saw firsthand "the efficacy of the offense." He admired "Scott's bold strategy and probably developed a confidence in attacking that made him miscalculate against an enemy well led and armed with rifles instead of much shorter-range muskets."[9]

Lee's most prominent critic in this regard has been Alan T. Nolan, whose widely read work leveled damning charges against the general's strategy and tactics. Following in the tradition of earlier writers such as George A. Bruce and J. F. C. Fuller, Nolan readily acknowledged Lee's brilliance as a field commander who won such dazzling victories as Second Manassas and Chancellorsville. But those offensive successes, coming at a prohibitively high cost in men and officers, typified an excessively aggressive style that drained the Confederacy's manpower and weakened its long-term prospects for independence. A Confederate defensive strategy characterized by carefully timed offensive counter-punches, averred Nolan, "would have kept its armies in the field long enough to wear down the North's willingness to carry on the war." Lee proved against Grant in Virginia that he could fight such a war, but his inclination always was to take the initiative and strike a blow. "When compared to the defensive," observed Nolan in summary, "Lee's offensive grand strategy, because of the losses entailed, led inexorably, to use his words, to the 'natural military consequences of the enemy's numerical superiority,' that is, surrender."[10]

The guerrilla option also postulates a defensive Confederate war, albeit one without large southern armies. Some historians have made remarkably optimistic pronouncements about how well a guerrilla scenario would have served the Confederacy. For example, Robert L. Kerby lambasted conservative southern political and military leaders who pigheadedly pursued a conventional war rather than a "war of national liberation" along the lines later made famous by "Mao, Che

Guevara, Fanon, Giap, Ho Chi Minh and others." Rather than mass conventional forces to defend all of its frontiers, the Confederacy should have emulated the American Revolution's example, "with a mobile-route army to cover her heartland, . . . as Washington covered the interior of the Middle States, and with the commitment of the remainder of her forces to hit-and-run harrying operations." Confederate soldiers remained local in their focus, claimed Kerby, continuing "to think like a militiaman or a guerrilla" even as their hidebound officers tried to turn them into professional soldiers. Also devoted to state rights and individual freedom, the civilian populace would have rallied behind a guerrilla war that kept men close to home. "Had the bulk of these 900,000 men been organized into local irregular units and commanded by captains as competent, ruthless and untrammeled by red tape as [William C.] Quantrill was," remarked Kerby, "they could have constituted one of the most formidable revolutionary armies in history."[11]

Drawing heavily on Kerby's analysis, Jeffrey Rogers Hummel's history of the Civil War sketched comparable benefits from a Confederate guerrilla war. Following the model of Americans who had fought a "war for national liberation . . . during their Revolution," the Confederacy should have organized and committed its manpower locally. "Although much of the South would have remained exposed to invasion," admitted Hummel, "Union willpower would have been patiently worn down through insurmountable logistical obstacles, continual hit and run harassment, and the countryside's implacable hostility." The problem lay in Richmond, where "the conservatives who had gained control of the

Confederate central government wished to establish a legitimate nation-state, not unleash a remorseless revolution." Hummel conceded that concern for controlling a huge slave population might have influenced the selection of a conventional strategy, but added that in pursuing that course the Confederacy "condemned itself to waging a war on the Union's terms."[12]

Other historians have raised the issue of a guerrilla option with less certainty while nonetheless labeling it the Confederacy's best route to independence. Richard Beringer and his colleagues asserted that as late as Appomattox guerrilla warfare could have defeated the North. Grant's strategy in 1864–65 had destroyed southern conventional forces, but it "provided no means of dealing with these armies should they disperse and thereafter continue offering organized resistance as units ranging in size from a division of several brigades down to independent companies." Like the Spanish who opposed Napoleon's soldiers a half-century earlier, these "units would have dominated the country, reducing Federal control to the immediate vicinity of Union armies." But white southerners lacked the devotion to the Confederacy necessary to risk a guerrilla war—"their one, otherwise invincible military weapon"—because the presence of millions of slaves meant that such a conflict could have unleashed a racial war such as that experienced by Santo Domingo. Reid Mitchell agreed that the Union probably could not "have won the war if the Confederacy had decided to wage it as a guerrilla war." Although many white southerners proved willing to do so, the Confederate government in 1861 opted for a conventional effort "because, in large part, it did not seem possible to fight a guerrilla war and keep slavery intact."[13]

Like Mitchell, John M. Gates noted that many Confederate leaders considered the thought of a guerrilla war abhorrent—a view shared by their northern counterparts. From the Federal perspective, a Confederate resistance comparable to that mounted by the Spaniards against Napoleon would have spawned intractable hatreds and made the process of reunion far more difficult. The North's "overwhelming superiority in both human and material resources" eventually wore the Confederacy down, and southern guerrilla operations never amounted to more than a peripheral problem that siphoned troops from invading Union armies to protect fragile lines of supply. Having laid out the reasons why a wide-scale people's war did not materialize in the Confederacy, Gates nonetheless opined that such a strategy "might have had a truly significant effect on events."[14]

The defensive war and guerrilla scenarios seem plausible from the sheltered confines of an academic dialogue. They likely would have conserved Confederate manpower and, by possibly lengthening the conflict, complicated the Lincoln government's task of keeping the northern population committed to subduing the rebellion. If subjected to the political, military, and social realities confronting Jefferson Davis, Lee, and other prominent leaders, however, a more purely defensive war or a guerrilla-based "war of liberation" wither as preferable alternatives to the actual Confederate effort. Southern military traditions in place as the Confederacy mobilized for fighting, civilian expectations in a democracy at war, the models of earlier wars to which white southerners looked for guidance, and the overwhelming imperative of maintaining white control in a slave-based society rendered both an overwhelmingly defensive strategy and a guerrilla resistance unacceptable. Neither would have garnered wide support in the civilian or the military sector, and thus it is inconceivable that either would have met the test of inspiriting white southerners for a protracted war.

Rather, the evidence supports the conclusion that a more narrowly defensive strategy was not well suited to Confederate expectations and would not necessarily have saved significant manpower or prolonged the war. Lee's aggressive strategy and tactics yielded immeasurably more good than evil for the southern nation. Guerrilla war was not a viable option within the Confederate context and thus should not be put forward in retrospect as the most desirable national strategy for the South.

Far too many historians play down or ignore entirely civilian expectations regarding the Confederacy's strategic posture. As citizens in a democratic republic, Confederates consistently made known their opinions about how the war was being conducted. Newspapers, diaries, and letters facilitate the reconstruction of those opinions, revealing a public overwhelmingly devoted to the idea of carrying the war to the enemy, holding on to or recapturing Confederate territory, and otherwise taking an offensive approach. Richmond diarist J. B. Jones commented in June 1861 that all signs pointed toward a defensive Confederate strategy for the initial year of the war. This policy "will be severely criticised," he affirmed, "for a vast majority of our people are for 'carrying the war into Africa' without a moment's delay. The sequel will show which is right, the government or the people. At all events," concluded Jones, "the government will rule."[15]

In the winter of 1861–62, before the string of disasters beginning with Fort Henry and culminating in the loss of Memphis beset Confederate arms in the Western Theater, the Richmond *Dispatch* characterized the "public mind" as "restless, and anxious to be relieved by some decisive action that shall have a positive influence in the progress of the war." The day before the opening of the Seven Days battles, J. B. Jones recorded that "our people are beginning to *fear* there will be no more fighting around Richmond until McClellan *digs* his way to it. The moment fighting ceases, our people have fits of gloom and despondency; but when they snuff battle in the breeze, they are animated with confidence." Several weeks later, a Macon, Georgia, newspaper expressed immense relief in conveying news of Lee's offensive movement toward the Potomac River and Maryland: "Having in this war exercised Christian forbearance to its utmost extent, by acting on the defensive, it will now be gratifying to all to see . . . the war carried upon the soil of those barbarians who have so long been robbing and murdering our quiet and unoffending citizens."[16]

Influential Richmond newspaper editor Edward A. Pollard, whose massive *Southern History of the War* chronicled the conflict as it unfolded, spoke directly to the question of the government's response to public expectations in 1862. Pollard chided Davis for being too timid strategically and accused him of an unwillingness "to consult the sentiment and wisdom of the people." Overly impressed with his own military ability, Davis thought it necessary "to dictate, from his cushioned seat in Richmond, the details of every campaign, and to conform every movement in the field to the invariable formula of *'the defensive policy.'*" Pollard's sarcastic allusion to a defensive strategy found an echo in a pair of diaries in early 1862. After drearily noting Confederate retreats in Kentucky, Tennessee, Louisiana, North Carolina, and Virginia, J. B. Jones recorded on May 14, "Our army has fallen back to within four miles of Richmond. Much anxiety is felt for the fate of the city. Is there no turning point in this long lane of downward progress?" Judith McGuire similarly charted retreats with a gloomy eye. "Our army has fallen back to the Rappahannock," she wrote on March 15, "thus giving up the splendid Valley and Piedmont country to the enemy. This, I suppose, is right, but it almost breaks our heart to think of it." Two months later McGuire reported people despondent as McClellan's army drew nearer to Richmond. The public heaped abuse on government officials: "Even General Lee does not escape animadversion, and the President is the subject of the most bitter maledictions."[17]

Dramatic fluctuations in Lee's reputation underscore the predilection for offensive action among the Confederate populace. Beginning the war as a figure from whom much was expected, Lee plummeted in the public's estimation following his service in western Virginia and along the South Atlantic coast during the fall and winter of 1861–62. Mary Chesnut reflected early hopes for Lee when she wrote in August 1861,

"We have repulsed them at Aquia Creek. If Gen. Lee only whips them in North West Virginia!" Shortly thereafter Chesnut mentioned a rumor that because of treacherous guides "a plan of Gen. Lee's for taking [William S.] Rosecrans had been frustrated." A month later she noted tersely that "[John B.] Floyd and Lee can not yet cope with [Jacob A.] Cox and Rosecrans." North Carolinian Catherine Edmondston reacted unfavorably to reports of Lee's assuming command of the Army of Northern Virginia after Joseph E. Johnston was wounded at Seven Pines. Earlier she had pronounced Lee an officer who was "too timid, believes too much in masterly inactivity, finds 'his strength' too much in 'sitting still.'" In early June 1862, Edmondston reiterated, in words repeated with slight variations in many quarters, "I do not much like him, he 'falls back' too much. He failed in Western Va owing, it was said, to the weather, has done little in the eyes of outsiders in S C. His nick name last summer was *old-stick-in-the-mud.*" She continued: "There is mud enough now in and about our lines, but pray God he may not fulfil the whole of his name."[18]

Edward Pollard harshly judged Lee in western Virginia as "a general who had never fought a battle . . . and whose extreme tenderness of blood induced him to depend exclusively upon the resources of strategy, to essay the achievement of victories without the cost of life." Pollard claimed that an "opportunity of a decisive battle in western Virginia was blindly lost, Gen. Lee making no attempt to follow up the enemy who had so skilfully eluded him." Armistead L. Long, who served on Lee's staff during the war, recalled the winter of 1861–62 as a time when the "press and the public were clamorous against" his superior; Edward Porter Alexander remembered that at the time Lee assumed army command "some of the newspapers—particularly the Richmond *Examiner*—pitched into him with extraordinary virulence," insisting that "henceforth our army would never be allowed to fight."[19]

Lee's strategic and tactical offensives from the Seven Days through the invasion of Maryland sent his stock soaring across the Confederacy, and Chancellorsville confirmed his position as the young nation's preeminent soldier. The Richmond *Dispatch* noted the speed with which the turnaround occurred. Eight days after the conclusion of the Seven Days, the paper observed, "The rise which this officer has suddenly taken in the public confidence is without precedent. At the commencement of the war he enjoyed the highest reputation of any officer on the continent. But his fame was considerably damaged by the result of his campaign over the mountains." The *Dispatch* had been among Lee's critics but now understood that the general had needed nothing but the proper stage on which to demonstrate his prowess. The Seven Days had supplied the stage, and Lee's offensive fighting against McClellan showcased his "great abilities." From a vantage point two years beyond Appomattox, Edward Pollard also remarked about Lee's fluctuating reputation during the war. Because "the Southern populace clamoured for bloody battles" and believed Lee was not a "fighting general" in late 1861, the Virginian may have been "the most unpopular commander of equal rank in the Confederate service" at that time. Lee's offensive successes, however, brought him to a point a few years later where he

....

"might have had the Dictatorship of the entire Southern Confederacy, if he had but crooked his finger to accept it."[20]

If Lee could be cast down in the public's estimation because of perceived timidity, it should come as no surprise that other commanders suffered similarly. Joseph E. Johnston will serve as an example. Lauded in much of the literature on Confederate military history as a wily officer who followed the dictates of the great Fabius in retreating masterfully, keeping his army intact, and surviving to fight another day, Johnston appeared to many of his contemporaries in a decidedly different light. They saw him as a general who refused to stand and fight, and who surrendered huge chunks of land virtually without a struggle. He retreated from Manassas Junction without a battle in the spring of 1862; gave up virtually all of the Peninsula in May 1862, crowding close to Richmond before finally confronting McClellan in the battle of Seven Pines; and fell back from near Chattanooga to the defenses of Atlanta in May and June 1864 without fighting a single major battle.

Such behavior eroded confidence among many Confederates. Writing shortly after the war, William P. Snow observed that Johnston's "continued retrograde movement" from Dalton to Atlanta in 1864 "naturally produced considerable disappointment and murmuring in the South." Three wartime witnesses suggest the type of complaints Johnston's nonaggressive generalship provoked. Speaking of the retreat toward Richmond in May 1862, a junior officer in Savannah, Georgia, stated that "General Johnston, from whom we were led to expect so much, has done little else than *evacuate,* until the very mention of the word sickens one *usque ad nauseam.*" This man thought Johnston's "doctrine of evacuation on every occasion . . . discourages our troops and people generally, and if persisted in must eventually contract our limits to an alarming extent." A soldier in the Army of Tennessee speculated that Jefferson Davis relieved Johnston in July 1864 "for not fighting and [for] allowing the Yanks to penetrate so far into Georgia." Less enamored of the general than previously, this man thought Johnston "too cautious, . . . not willing to risk a battle until he is satisfied he can whip it." A young South Carolina woman commented bitterly about Johnston late in the war. "The last news from Johnston was that he had retreated to Raleigh," she wrote. "This arch-retreater will probably retreat till perhaps he retreats to Gen. Lee, who may put a stop to his retrograde movement."[21]

Results on the battlefield lent credence to widespread sentiment in favor of mounting at least some major offensive operations. Defensive strategy often yielded meager long-term results or exposed territory to invaders (territory usually owned by Confederate voters). Most disastrously for the Confederacy, defensive operations sometimes culminated in sieges. Albert Sidney Johnston's static defense of the Kentucky–Tennessee front in 1861–62 resulted in the surrender of some 15,000 soldiers at Fort Donelson as well as the loss of Nashville and crucial agricultural and industrial production in Middle Tennessee. During the spring and early summer of 1863, Joseph E. Johnston and John C. Pemberton presided over another defensive fiasco that cost the Confederacy an entire army at Vicksburg. Again shunning any attempt to gain the strategic initiative when Sherman advanced against Atlanta, Johnston retreated to that city's defenses to begin a siege that also ended in Union triumph (the Confederacy was fortunate that its western army escaped capture). Had Johnston not been wounded at Seven Pines, his withdrawal up the Peninsula toward Richmond in 1862 almost certainly would have ended in another siege and, most probably, the loss of Richmond to George B. McClellan's investing army.

Indeed, every significant siege of the war—all of which closed campaigns wherein Confederates held the strategic defensive—brought Union victory. That list included the siege of Petersburg, which ended as Lee had predicted it would in June 1864. Speaking to Jubal Early after the battle of Cold Harbor, Lee stated, "We must destroy this army of Grant's before he gets to [the] James River. If he gets there, it will become a siege, and then it will be a mere question of time."[22]

When manpower lost through the capitulation of besieged forces is factored into the relative cost of offensive and defensive strategies, the latter look far less attractive than many historians would have it. Even leaving aside surrendered troops, strategically defensive campaigns often drained manpower at a rate almost equal to that lost by the side on the offensive. The problem lay in the fact that defenders usually reached a point where they had to attack in order to avoid a siege. At the same time, these tactical counteroffensives were fraught with challenges that often militated against success.

Three examples illustrate this point. The Confederates lost more men than their opponents when Joseph E. Johnston retreated up the Peninsula in May 1862. In the delaying action at Williamsburg and at Seven Pines, where Johnston took the tactical offensive because McClellan's army had reached the outskirts of Richmond, southern casualties totaled nearly 8,000 to fewer than 7,500 for the Federals. Similarly, during the first seventeen days of May 1863, Grant pursued the strategic offensive in Mississippi, fighting aggressive battles at Port Gibson, Raymond, and Jackson. With Federal forces approaching Vicksburg from the west, John C. Pemberton attacked them unsuccessfully at Champion Hill. A Confederate rear-guard action followed at the Big Black River before the armies settled into a siege at Vicksburg. During this prelude to siege operations, Pemberton and Joseph E. Johnston lost nearly 6,000 men, Grant just more than 4,300.[23] Finally, in May 1864, during Johnston's withdrawal across north Georgia toward Atlanta, Confederates lost roughly 10,000 men to Sherman's 11,768.[24]

Lee conducted perhaps the most famous strategic defense of the war in May and June 1864. In defending the Rappahannock, North Anna, and Chickahominy river lines against Grant's relentless offensive, Lee's army suffered proportionately higher losses than the Federals—despite the fact that it usually fought from behind excellent field works. Regarding this campaign, McWhiney and Jamieson remarked that "Lee was at his best on defense," conducting a brilliant fighting withdrawal that "made the Union pay in manpower as it had never paid before." They neglect to mention that Lee's army also was paying as it never had paid before, losing more than 30,000 men between the initial engagement in the Wilderness and the movement across the James River six weeks later.[25]

Many historians have used the battle of Fredericksburg to show how Confederates could overcome Union numbers by fighting from a strong defensive position. Alan T. Nolan called it "Lee's most intelligent and well-fought battle during 1862 and 1863." For once, the combative general did not engage in "an inevitably costly offensive campaign," suppressing "his risky and Napoleonic bent, his costly aggressiveness" and avoiding "the massive and disproportionate casualties that frequently marked his battles." McWhiney and Jamieson also discussed Lee's easy success at Fredericksburg, emphasizing that Burnside's mismanaged attacks "ended in disaster."[26] But what lessons should be learned from Lee's effortless success in mid-December 1862? Unless the North proved so inept as to send a procession of bumbling army commanders against the Confederates, the chances of replicating the experience at Fredericksburg were very slim.

That fact stood out when Lee faced the first major post-Fredericksburg Union offensive. In late April 1863, his soldiers waited behind strong lines at Fredericksburg as Joseph Hooker maneuvered the Army of the Potomac along the left bank of the Rappahannock River. Never contemplating a direct assault against Lee, Hooker executed a skillful strategic turning movement against the southern left. Lee responded by seizing the tactical initiative, flanking Hooker's troops west of Chancellorsville, and winning his most famous victory. Although Confederate losses were heavy at Chancellorsville, the alternative would have been to retreat southward, take up a position behind the North Anna River or elsewhere, and hope for a chance to strike the Federals there. Lee opted to hit Hooker while the Federal army was divided, with Hooker's main body at Chancellorsville and a smaller force under John Sedgwick at Fredericksburg. Confronting the enemy in detail, Lee earned a victory that depressed northern morale, inspired men and officers within the Army of Northern Virginia, and persuaded many Confederates that Lee and his army were invincible.[27]

Chancellorsville affords just one example of why Lee's aggressive battles must be evaluated with an eye toward more than their human cost. Critics emphasize casualties—often relative Confederate and Union casualties—to prove that his offensive operations extracted too high a price. Thus Alan T. Nolan observed that "at Chancellorsville, a victory, Lee lost 13,000 of 61,000 effectives, more than 21 percent, a much higher percentage than that suffered by the Federals." In a similar vein, and with an indifferent grasp of the numbers involved, Thomas L. Connelly claimed that "Lee lost more men at Chancellorsville than the Confederates surrendered at Forts Henry and Donelson combined in 1862."[28] Lee's storied battles in 1862–63 did deplete southern manpower at a rapid rate—cumulative casualties from the Seven Days, Second Manassas, the Antietam campaign, Fredericksburg, and Chancellorsville approached 65,000, of whom more than 10,000 were killed in action and another several thousand likely died from wounds or were permanently disabled.[29] But historians should probe beyond casualties. Did this effusion of blood translate into a net gain for the Confederacy? Would a defensive posture have accomplished as much? Did Lee's campaigns in 1862–63 bring the Confederacy closer to independence?

Lee's battles during his first year in command of the Army of Northern Virginia undoubtedly advanced the Confederate cause. The Seven Days ended a period of several months when only Stonewall Jackson's small victories in the Shenandoah Valley had broken a spell of defeat in the Western Theater, in the Trans-Mississippi, and along the Atlantic coast. Between June 1 and September 1, 1862, Lee's offensive victories at the Seven Days and Second Manassas drastically reoriented the war in Virginia. On June 1, McClellan's huge army stood just outside Richmond, and another formidable northern force lay at Fredericksburg. If Joseph E. Johnston had remained in command, McClellan likely would have besieged and taken the Confederate capital that summer. That blow, coming after the loss of Middle Tennessee, New Orleans, Memphis, Corinth, and other important points probably would have sealed the Confederacy's fate. But by September 1, Lee's victories had cleared Virginia of Federal armies and taken the war to the banks of the Potomac River. Confederate civilian morale rebounded, European leaders concluded the South was winning the war, and Lincoln faced a crisis with northern elections looming in November. Apart from these rich psychological and political dividends, Virginia's farmers were able to gather a harvest vital to Confederate logistical planning.

Lee's victories at Fredericksburg and Chancellorsville sent another series of shock waves through the North. "My God! my God!" agonized Lincoln after Chancellorsville: "What will the country say?" Senator Charles Sumner of Massachusetts answered for many northerners when he blurted out to Secretary of the Navy Gideon Welles, "Lost, lost, all is lost." One careful historian observed that the "Union army had again suffered a bitter blow to its morale, and the North was once more sunk in discouragement"—a situation arising from Lee's apparent mastery of the generals who commanded the Army of the Potomac.[30]

On the Confederate side, Chancellorsville crystallized Lee's image as his nation's chief hope. The battle "made Lee immortal in the minds of his men," commented a leading student of Confederate military affairs, and many of the general's fellow citizens described him thereafter as an "invincible" commander who had never been beaten.[31] James M. McPherson asserted that the boost Chancellorsville gave to Lee's soldiers "proved in the end harmful, for it bred an overconfidence in their own prowess and a contempt for the enemy that led to disaster" at Gettysburg. Moreover, noted McPherson, "Southern elation over the victory at Chancellorsville masked intensifying problems for the Confederacy," including a tightening blockade, rampant inflation, and Union military gains along the Mississippi River and in Tennessee.[32]

McPherson correctly identified the impact of Lee's victory inside and outside his army but overlooked one important factor. Battles such as Chancellorsville promulgated a faith in Lee and his soldiers that sustained civilian morale during later difficult times, helping Confederates cope with the blockade, a devalued currency, and Union victories outside Virginia because they retained hope for independence and an end to their travails. The long-term value of Lee's incontrovertibly bloody offensive triumphs in 1862–63 showed most dramatically during the summer of 1864. Northern will crumbled under the pressure of immense casualty lists from the Overland campaign and the grinding stalemate of sieges at Richmond/Petersburg and Atlanta, prompting Lincoln's famous memorandum in which he prophesied Republican defeat in November 1864. Confederate confidence in Lee and his army, in contrast, suffered little if any erosion. The aura of success surrounding the Army of Northern Virginia as a result of Lee's first year in command remained firmly in place, as it would through the rest of 1864 and into 1865. Thus could a European visitor to the Confederacy report in March 1865 that Lee was "the idol of his soldiers & the Hope of His country." This witness pronounced "the almost fanatical belief in his judgement & capacity" to be "the one idea of an entire people."[33]

Lee's bartering thousands of lives for victories during 1862–63 made the Army of Northern Virginia a highly visible symbol of Confederate nationalism. Civilians and soldiers alike rallied to that symbol, persisting in their struggle for independence long past the point at which a cold calculation of resources and probabilities would have dictated capitulation. Without Lee's aggressive, forward-moving strategy, few, if any— and certainly no major—Confederate victories would have been possible. Likewise, no consistently strong and sustained sense of nationalism and determined will on the part of the Confederate people could have been imaginable without at least occasional good news from the battlefield.

The concept of a massive guerrilla war as the Confederate national strategy is even more far-fetched than a determinedly defensive one.

Such a policy would have required white southerners to repudiate their obvious military leaders in 1861, embrace a type of war at best marginally related to their martial tradition and for which they felt no affinity, and, most important, accept the risk of disrupting their social and economic control over 3.5 million enslaved black people. Except as an academic exercise in applying twentieth-century lessons to a nineteenth-century example, debate over the merits of a "people's war" has scant relevance to the Confederacy.

Jefferson Davis supplied the opening for historians to broach the subject of guerrilla war. On April 4, 1865, he addressed the Confederate citizenry about the need to fight on despite the fall of Richmond two days earlier. "We have now entered upon a new phase of a struggle," stated Davis, "the memory of which is to endure for all ages, and to shed ever increasing lustre upon our country." In the president's view, the loss of Richmond and other major cities rendered "our army free to move from point to point, and strike in detail the detachments and garrisons of the enemy; operating in the interior of our own country, where supplies are more accessible, and where the foe will be far removed from his own base, and cut off from all succor in case of reverse." If Confederates retained their "unquenchable resolve," this new style of war would bring victory and independence. For those enamored of the guerrilla option, Davis's address has seemed to indicate that he belatedly recognized the merits of such a national strategy. One historian remarked that Davis's words "could have been uttered by Mao Tse-tung or Ho Chi Minh," adding that modern students could "only wonder what prodigies of determination such rhetoric would have inspired in 1861, when the people of the South were still flushed with enthusiasm."[34]

Often overlooked in this address is Davis's explicit mention of Lee and the Army of Northern Virginia. When the president alluded to "our army" he meant Lee's force: "For many months the largest and finest army of the Confederacy, under the command of a leader whose presence inspires equal confidence in the troops and the people, has been greatly trammeled by the necessity of keeping constant watch over the approaches to the capital, and has thus been forced to forego more than one opportunity for promising enterprises." Davis envisioned not so much a twentieth-century style "people's war" as an unleashed Army of Northern Virginia taking the offensive against whatever pieces of the Federal army it could find.[35]

Even this strategy fell on deaf ears at Lee's headquarters. The Confederate commander surrendered the Army of Northern Virginia rather than trying to adapt it to some type of quasi-guerrilla operations. The latter use would bring anarchy, Lee told an artillerist just before Appomattox, because the soldiers "would have no rations & they would be under no discipline . . . They would have to plunder & rob to procure subsistence. The country would be full of lawless bands in every part, & a state of society would ensue from which it would take the country years to recover." Eleven days after he and Grant met at Appomattox, Lee told Davis substantially the same thing. No army could be "organized or supported" in Virginia, no part of the Confederacy east of the

Mississippi offered any better prospects, and a guerrilla war would bring nothing but misery. "A partisan war may be continued, and hostilities protracted, causing individual suffering and the devastation of the country," argued Lee, "but I see no prospect by that means of achieving a separate independence."[36]

Nor would announcement of such a strategy in 1861 have prompted an enthusiastic response. As a group, Lee, Albert Sidney Johnston, Joseph E. Johnston, P. G. T. Beauregard, and other West Point–trained Confederate military leaders had won numerous brevets for gallantry and merit during the war with Mexico and had held prominent positions in the late antebellum United States army. They represented an ideal of the gentleman as military officer that held great appeal in the antebellum South, where schools such as the Virginia Military Institute, the South Carolina Military Academy (the Citadel), and other less famous institutions had been structured to produce graduates in the mold of West Pointers. Many antebellum white southerners believed that men educated at VMI and other military schools would form a valuable pool of available leaders to serve their states and region should sectional tensions result in open conflict. Thus did the featured speaker at the 1850 dedication of a new cadet barracks at VMI allude to "the portentous cloud gathering in the North" during remarks that, according to one historian of the school, sounded the theme "In peace prepare for war."[37] Considering the efforts to replicate West Point in schools in their own states, it is inconceivable that white southerners facing possible northern invasion would have shunned prominent West Pointers—virtually all of whom probably would have considered a guerrilla war anathema—in favor of unknown and untried men who would command small bands of partisans.[38]

Moreover, for the younger southern officers, many of whom were thoroughly infused with Confederate nationalism, the meaning of soldierly duty meant a traditional military command, a disciplined army, and the goal of final victory on the field of battle—not a desperate resort to guerrilla warfare. These were the men who formed the core of strength in Lee's army and in every other Confederate force of any substance throughout the war, reflecting and fulfilling the larger public devotion to the Confederate cause until the end of the conflict.

Guerrilla war also would have been inappropriate for the kind of nation Confederates hoped to establish. They envisioned taking their place among the roster of recognized western states, a goal that demanded creation of the requisite formal governmental institutions. In his inaugural address, Jefferson Davis spoke to his fellow citizens of "the position which we have assumed among the nations of the earth." The president observed that "as a consequence of our new condition and relations . . . it will be necessary to provide for the speedy and efficient organization of branches of the Executive department having special charge of foreign intercourse, finance, military affairs, and the postal service." The new nation could not rely on the various state militias: "In the present condition of affairs, . . . there should be a well-instructed and disciplined army, more numerous than would usually be required for a peace establishment."[39]

Confederate leaders understood that French intervention had tipped the balance in favor of the colonists during the American Revolution.[40] European recognition and possible intervention also could prove decisive in the Confederacy's struggle for nationhood. Davis's use of the adjectives "well-instructed and disciplined" to describe the southern army revealed his grasp of a crucial factor in persuading European leaders that the Confederacy was more than an amorphous collection of insurrectionaries. Would Great Britain and France have contemplated extending recognition to a fledgling Confederacy that relied on guerrilla units rather than on a formal army? Would harassment of Federal armies, rather than victories such as Lee's in 1862 and 1863, have persuaded Europeans that the Confederacy seemed destined to achieve independence—as Saratoga had pointed the way toward American independence in 1777?

William E. Gladstone's oft-quoted speech at Newcastle in October 1862 underscored the importance of the institutional trappings of nationhood. Whatever one's attitude toward the South and slavery, insisted Gladstone, "there is no doubt that Jefferson Davis and other leaders of the South have made an army; they are making, it appears, a navy; and they have made what is more than either—they have made a nation." The key lay in battlefield triumphs won by national armies. Following Lee's victories at the Seven Days and Second Manassas, Great Britain's Prime Minister Palmerston and Foreign Secretary Lord Russell concluded that the North could not defeat the Confederacy. Britain and France should recommend an end to the conflict on the basis of separation; if the North refused to negotiate, wrote Russell to Palmerston on September 17, "we ought ourselves to recognise the Southern States as an independent State." Although Lee's repulse at Antietam prompted the British to back away from recognition, that should not obscure how close the Confederates had come to persuading Europe of their viability as a nation. "By mid-1862 the Palmerston ministry in London had moved close to an intervention," concluded one historian of the war's diplomatic front, "that doubtless would have led to recognition and a third Anglo-American war."[41]

Supporters of the guerrilla option for the Confederacy often cite the importance of the American Revolution as a model but emphasize the wrong dimension of that earlier struggle. Although colonial militias and partisan leaders—including southerners such as Francis Marion and Thomas Sumter—had earned success in the campaigns of the Revolution, Confederates looked to George Washington, who always placed the broad interests of the nascent nation above local needs, and the Continental Army, which loomed large in the memory of Saratoga, Yorktown, and other benchmark military events, as their models. P. G. T. Beauregard, the hero of Sumter and First Manassas, wrote in the summer of 1861 that "Washington and the Revolution should always be present in our minds. He never desponded, and hence he finally triumphed." The Confederate Congress adopted a Great Seal featuring a mounted Washington, the postal department issued stamps with his likeness, and citizens frequently mentioned Lee and Washington as pillars of their respective causes. Typical of Confederates who connected Washington and Lee, Mary Jones expressed gratitude in December 1862 that "the head of our army is a noble son of Virginia, and worthy of the intimate relation in which he stands connected with our immortal Washington." Writing in 1865 after Lee had achieved his full stature as a Confederate hero, Eliza Andrews invoked the obvious comparison in calling him "that star of light before which even Washington's glory pales."[42]

Early adoption of a guerrilla strategy would have entailed other potential problems. The immediate concession of considerable territory to the Federals would have alienated thousands of citizens. As Russell F. Weigley observed, the Richmond government experienced intense pressure to defend territory: "No part of the Confederacy's frontiers, except possibly parts of the trans-Mississippi West, was so undeveloped and so lacking in political influence that President Davis could afford to be . . . cavalier . . . about the central government's contributions to local defense." Allan R. Millett and Peter Maslowski agreed, correctly observing that "states' rights oratory aside, all the southern states wanted the national government to bear the major defense burden."[43] Overall, very little evidence suggests that Confederate citizens would have embraced a strategy predicated on the need to surrender huge pieces of territory in return for opportunities to strike vulnerable elements of the Union army.

And what of the problem of maintaining national morale? A guerrilla war could erode Union will only as long as the Confederate populace remained firmly devoted to the effort. Irregular units could not have supplied battlefield victories of the magnitude Lee's army won in 1862 and 1863. Nor is it easy to imagine that any partisan leader could have achieved the stature of Lee. Absent Lee and his famous victories, it is difficult to imagine what would have bolstered civilian morale in the midst of brutal combat typical of the war in Missouri and in other areas where conventional armies played secondary roles. There would have been no sense of building toward victory and independence, and citizens likely would have lost heart amid the chaos and blood that so demoralized Missourians. Michael Fellman's incisive study of Missouri indicated that irregular fighting spun out of control. "Guerrilla warfare blew the cover off respectable society, and undermined official values," wrote Fellman. "No official response could end or even deflect the self-governing engines of guerrilla war." Missouri suffered all that Lee sought to avoid in calling for surrender rather than a shift toward guerrilla fighting: brutality and reprisal with no compensating progress toward Confederate independence.[44]

The threat of such chaos in a slave-based society stood as the most important obstacle to a Confederate policy of guerrilla war. John Brown's raid on Harpers Ferry in October 1859 had raised the specter of white northerners invading the South with the purpose of inciting slave insurrection. A series of fires in Texas attributed to abolitionists in the summer of 1860, together with that year's highly charged presidential election, aggravated an already volatile climate within which rumors of slave revolts spread rapidly and triggered repressive measures. Based on a close investigation of reaction to the events in Texas, Donald

Reynolds concluded that "hangings and whippings that occurred during the summer of 1860 make it clear that in the aftermath of the Texas fires the South experienced one of the greatest witch hunts in American history." Clarence L. Mohr's detailed treatment of slavery in wartime Georgia demonstrated that the repercussions of Harpers Ferry and the Texas fires continued well past the secession crisis: "Throughout most of 1861 black Georgians lived in an atmosphere of hostility and suspicion which differed little from that of the preceding summer." White Georgians manifested a double-edged fear—the war might entail a loss of slave property and, more ominously, no one could tell how "slaves would respond to a war with the 'abolitionist' North."[45]

Once fighting began, the approach of Union forces inevitably provoked alarm among white southerners about the consequences for their slaves. A young woman in Fredericksburg, Virginia, voiced common concerns about loss of property and potential insurrection as Federal troops occupied the vicinity in April 1862. "The negroes are going off in great numbers, and are beginning to be very independent and impudent," wrote Betty Herndon Maury. "We hear that our three are going soon. I am afraid of the lawless Yankee soldiers, but that is nothing to my fear of the negroes if they should rise against us." In his study of the occupied Confederacy, Steven V. Ash observed that, although "inclined to yield without a fight to Federal occupation, most citizens in the invaded regions remained resolutely determined to subjugate the enemies in their midst." Those "enemies" included slaves, who suffered increased restrictions on their movements and activities.

The magistrates of Pasquotank County, North Carolina, reacted in typical fashion, calling out the local militia in February 1862 not to fight the Yankees who had entered Albemarle Sound, but to increase slave patrols.[46]

Both late antebellum fears of insurrection and behavior when confronting Union invaders during the war strongly suggest that white southerners would not have countenanced a national guerrilla strategy in 1861. Such a strategy would have accelerated the process by which slaves came into contact with Federal armies, thereby subjecting the Confederate social structure to massive pressure. Having opted for secession in large measure to protect their slave-based society, it strains credulity to believe Confederates would have selected a strategy calculated to undermine their economic and social control over millions of enslaved black people.

In another important regard guerrilla war was not a viable national strategy. Steven Ash's analysis of the occupied South contradicts the thesis that hundreds of thousands of Confederates would have joined small militia forces or irregular units in a massive popular resistance against Yankee invaders. Some Confederates in occupied regions "thought organized partisan warfare could significantly disrupt larger enemy forces," remarked Ash. In some areas the call went out for volunteers to fight the Federals, but results were disappointing: "Almost without exception, such efforts to rally citizen forces failed. Although a few individuals grabbed their guns and headed into the woods determined to fight a guerrilla war, the citizenry as a whole declined to resist invasion by force of arms." Ash worked with a population from which Confederate soldiers and many civilian and military leaders already had been removed, so conclusions based on his work must be tentative. Still, the overwhelming rejection of guerrilla warfare he described cannot be dismissed.[47]

Proponents of the guerrilla option overlook a final crucial point. Successful people's wars almost always have benefited from dependable outside support. John Ellis, having reviewed more than 150 internal struggles, pointed out that in cases where the guerrillas triumphed "the issue was rarely decided in terms of the military confrontation between the insurgents and the incumbents." Among factors beyond the guerrillas' own military strength, "one of the most common . . . was that the guerrillas had the *direct or indirect aid of regular troops*." The French supplied that aid to the colonists during the American Revolution, the British to the Spanish guerrillas fighting Napoleon, and the Chinese to the North Vietnamese and Viet Cong contending against the Americans in Vietnam, to name but three instances.[48] Who could have stepped in to help the Confederates? Certainly not the British. And however much Napoleon III might have appreciated Confederate recognition of his puppet regime in Mexico, the French never would have risked unilateral military intervention in the American conflict. The Confederacy had no potential ally, a circumstance that would have limited severely its ability to wage a winning partisan war.

In early May 1863, Jefferson Davis wrote a brief letter to his brother Joseph in which he discussed military affairs. Davis understood that his brother worried about the defense of their home state of Mississippi. The president called Earl Van Dorn's recent withdrawal from northern Mississippi "one of those blunders which it is difficult to compensate for." The just completed battle of Chancellorsville, in contrast, had been "a great victory, in view of the thorough preparation of the Enemy and his superiority of numbers, not less than two to one." With Lee's performance along the Rappahannock obviously in mind, the president alluded to his inability to find other capable commanders who would give the nation that type of morale-building news. "A *General* in the full acceptation of the word is a rare product, scarcely more than one can be expected in a generation," observed Davis, "but in this mighty war in which we are engaged there is need for half a dozen." Nine months earlier, he had made this same point to Francis W. Pickens when he remarked that "a great General is so rare that their names mark the arch of history."[49]

Davis's two statements highlight a major component of the Confederacy's failure to win independence. The Davis administration pursued a national strategy calculated both to satisfy the expectations and needs of the citizenry and to advance the cause of Confederate independence, but among the South's field commanders only Lee carved a record destined for commemoration on Davis's "arch of history." Although Lee and the Army of Northern Virginia waged campaigns that more than once brought independence within sight, no other general stepped forward to make a comparable contribution.[50] When the North finally found a pair of superior army commanders in Grant and Sherman, the

Confederacy proved able to counter only with Lee. The final failure lay not so much with Confederate strategy as with the men available to Davis to carry it out.

The factors underlying that Confederate failure have mesmerized historians for too long. The time is ripe to consider the more complex and fruitful question of why white southerners fought as long as they did. The interplay among popular expectations, national strategy, performance on the battlefield, and Confederate nationalism and will offers rich opportunities for investigation. Only by seeking to understand why the Confederacy endured as long as it did will scholars explain why hundreds of thousands of men served steadfastly in Confederate armies, supported by a majority of their friends and neighbors behind the lines, and why soldiers and civilians developed a sense of nationalism and exhibited a will to succeed that very nearly established a slaveholding republic.

Black Union soldiers march past smoking ruins along Main Street in Richmond on April 3, 1865. The spectacle of former slaves, armed and wearing United States uniforms, entering their capital under the Stars and Stripes proved especially galling to many Confederates, one of whom wrote bitterly: "Long lines of negro cavalry swept by the Exchange Hotel, brandishing their swords and uttering savage cheers, replied to by the shouts of those of their own color, who were trudging along under loads of plunder, laughing and exulting over the prizes they had secured from the wreck of the stores, rather than rejoicing at the more precious prize of freedom which had been won for them." (*Frank Leslie's Illustrated Newspaper,* April 29, 1865)

The human toll for the Confederacy was staggering—one quarter of its 1860 military-age white males killed and another quarter maimed. These dead were among thousands who fell during fighting near Spotsylvania Court House, Virginia, in May 1864. (Francis Trevelyan Miller, ed., *The Photographic History of the Civil War,* 10 vols. New York: Review of Reviews, 1911, 3:61

Graves of soldiers buried hastily near where they had fallen offered another reminder of the war's cost. Most of the remains could not be identified when later reinterred in southern cemeteries. In the spring of 1862, a Union photographer made this study of rough wooden markers over graves of soldiers killed eight months earlier in the battle of First Manassas. (Francis Trevelyan Miller, ed., *The Photographic History of the Civil War,* 10 vols. New York: Review of Reviews, 1911, 9:278)

The Confederacy's economic infrastructure suffered severe damage during the war. Victorious Federals posing with a destroyed Confederate locomotive in Richmond symbolize the North's triumph over an economically ravaged South. (Francis Trevelyan Miller, ed., *The Photographic History of the Civil War*, 10 vols. New York: Review of Reviews, 1911, 9:324)

Confederate armies had caused some of the economic destruction that surrounded white southerners at the close of the war. John Bell Hood's Army of Tennessee set fire to an ordnance train as it withdrew from Atlanta. The resulting explosions wrecked not only the railroad cars but also a large rolling mill that stood alongside the tracks. (Francis Trevelyan Miller, ed., *The Photographic History of the Civil War,* 10 vols. New York: Review of Reviews, 1911, 3:135)

The stark shell of the massive Gallego flour mills produced a ghostly reflection along the Richmond waterfront shortly after the city fell. Retreating Confederates had burned the armory, arsenal, and other structures, and flames engulfed much of the city before Federal troops arrived. Diarist John B. Jones wrote on April 3, 1865: "Some of the great flour mills have taken fire from the burning government warehouses, and the flames are spreading through the lower part of the city. A great conflagration is apprehended." (Francis Trevelyan Miller, ed., *The Photographic History of the Civil War,* 10 vols. New York: Review of Reviews, 1911, 9:306)

The Virginia state capitol, which had housed the Confederate Congress for most of the war, rises forlornly above a block of gutted buildings in Richmond. (Library of Congress)

Two women in mourning clothing walk among the ruins of Richmond in April 1865—a tableau duplicated at innumerable southern sites. (Francis Trevelyan Miller, ed., *The Photographic History of the Civil War,* 10 vols. New York: Review of Reviews, 1911, 9:231)

View of Columbia, South Carolina, from the state capitol. Few Confederate cities presented a more ravaged appearance as the war drew to a close. (Francis Trevelyan Miller, ed., *The Photographic History of the Civil War,* 10 vols. New York: Review of Reviews, 1911, 3:240)

The southern countryside, as in this area near Centreville, Virginia, also bore marks of the conflict where armies had left a desolate landscape stripped of vegetation and scarred by earthworks. (National Archives)

Wrecked private homes served as yet another reminder of the war's toll on Confederate society. Among the first to suffer this fate was Judith Henry's modest dwelling on the battlefield of First Manassas, reduced to a crumbling chimney and fragments of wood framing when photographed in 1862. (Francis Trevelyan Miller, ed., *The Photographic History of the Civil War,* 10 vols. New York: Review of Reviews, 1911, 9:85)

Confronted with overwhelming physical evidence of their defeat, former Confederates sought to honor their failed struggle for independence. This 90-foot granite pyramid in Richmond's Hollywood Cemetery, completed in November 1869, was among the first monuments to soldiers who had died in Confederate service. Between June 1872 and October 1873, nearly 3,000 Confederate dead were disinterred from the Gettysburg battlefield and reburied in the shadow of this pyramid. (Eleanor S. Brockenbrough Library, The Museum of the Confederacy, Richmond, Virginia; copied by Katherine Wetzel)

Thousands of former Confederates attended the May 1890 dedication of this monumental equestrian statue of Robert E. Lee in Richmond. Together with Confederate memorial day services and speeches at funerals of prominent ex-Confederates, ceremonies at such unveilings helped keep alive well into the twentieth century memories of the South's struggle for independence. (Eleanor S. Brockenbrough Library, The Museum of the Confederacy, Richmond, Virginia; copied by Katherine Wetzel)

4

DEFEAT

"What else could we do but give up?"

The Confederacy capitulated in the spring of 1865 because northern armies had demonstrated their ability to crush organized southern military resistance. Soldiers laid down their arms at Appomattox and Durham Station when brought to bay by imposing Federal forces under the resolute command of U. S. Grant and William Tecumseh Sherman. Civilians who had maintained faith in their defenders despite material hardship and social disruption similarly recognized that the end had come. Confederates in and out of uniform did not reconcile easily to this harsh reality and would have preferred a peace with southern independence, but they accepted what seemed to them the unequivocal verdict of the battlefield. The North had vanquished southern armies and thereby settled the questions of secession and emancipation. Although some white southerners had remained more steadfast than others and a significant number never had given their hearts to the cause, most Confederates knew that as a people they had expended blood and treasure in profusion before ultimately collapsing in the face of northern power sternly applied. Later they would fashion a public memory of the war that gave meaning to their unimaginable loss and bitter defeat, but in April and May 1865 they realistically suppressed all thoughts of large-scale resort to arms.[1]

Testimony from the aftermath of the war reveals unequivocally that most Confederates believed they had been beaten rather than undermined by internal weaknesses. The first sentence of Lee's famous farewell address to his soldiers conveyed this attitude: "After four years of arduous service, marked by unsurpassed courage and fortitude, the Army of Northern Virginia has been compelled to yield to overwhelming numbers and resources." Catherine Edmondston and Sarah Hine typified those who seconded Lee's assessment that the North had overpowered Confederate defenders in the field. North Carolinian Edmondston, who repeatedly had vowed to resist to the bitter end, remarked in her diary that "the Vulgar Yankee nation exults over our misfortunes, places its foot upon our necks, & extols its own prowess in conquering us. They command all the R Roads & other routes of travel & they have the ability to force their detested oath down the throat of every man amongst us."[2]

Georgian Sarah Hine hated the idea of relinquishing hope for an independent Confederacy but had no doubt about what had compelled Confederate surrender. "One thing I shall glory in to the latest hour of my life," she wrote, is that "we never yielded in the struggle until we were bound hand & foot & the heel of the despot was on our throats." What was the condition of those who yielded to the Federals? "Bankrupt in men, in money, & in provisions," explained Hine, "the wail of the bereaved & the cry of hunger rising all over the land, Our cities burned with fire and our pleasant things laid waste, the best & bravest of our sons in captivity, and the entire resources of our country exhausted—what else could we do but give up."[3]

Graphic evidence supporting Hine's stark catalog greeted anyone traveling through the South after the Confederate surrender. Thousands of graves bespoke the grim toll on a generation of young men. Many of the dead had been interred hastily near where they had fallen, their remains often subject to the ravages of rooting hogs or the elements. Visiting the battlefield at the Wilderness shortly after the war, northern writer John T. Trowbridge described "three or four Rebel graves with old headboards" near a fence corner. "The words indicated that those buried were North Carolinians," observed Trowbridge: "The graves were shallow, and the settling of the earth over the bodies had left the feet of one of the poor fellows sticking out."[4] Uncertainty about the location of dead relatives heightened the pain of loss in countless southern households, and ubiquitous empty sleeves and trouser legs afforded additional reminders of sacrifice in a brutal war.

Major southern cities bore deep scars from the conflict. Photographer George N. Barnard, who followed the route of Sherman's army across Georgia and through the Carolinas, recorded ruined private homes, burned railroad yards, and piles of rubble that once had been public buildings in Atlanta, Columbia, and Charleston. In Richmond, where Confederates had set fire to public facilities as they retreated, photographers trained their cameras on scenes in the vicinity of the state capitol (which had housed the Confederate Congress during most of the war), near the Tredegar Iron Works, and among huge mills along the James River. Their haunting images captured the widespread devastation described by war clerk John B. Jones after a walk through the ruined section of Richmond on April 4, 1865. "Some seven hundred houses, from Main Street to the canal, comprising the most valuable stores, and the best business establishments," stated Jones, "were consumed. All the bridges across the James were destroyed, the work being done effectually."[5] Hundreds of miles of trenches, once occupied by Union and Confederate soldiers seeking shelter from minié balls and artillery projectiles, formed ugly rings around such cities as Petersburg, Richmond, Chattanooga, Atlanta, and Vicksburg, and long sections of field works similarly marred the rural southern landscape.

In addition to the serpentine lines of field works, physical damage comparable to anything in the cities extended across vast stretches of the agricultural South. Wherever armies had camped for any length of time, thousands of hungry campfires had devoured many acres of forests, substituting moonscapes for previously lush vegetation. Long before William Tecumseh Sherman and Philip H. Sheridan struck at logistical production in central Georgia and the Shenandoah Valley during their famous 1864 campaigns (operations often cited by historians to mark the beginning of a harsher phase of war), much of the Confederacy's farming heartland already had experienced catastrophic damage from armies bent on destruction or merely seeking food and fodder for thousands of soldiers and animals.

A half dozen witnesses from Virginia, Tennessee, and Louisiana suggest the degree of civilian dislocation. British observer A. J. L. Fremantle noted in June 1863 that the region along the eastern slope of the Blue Ridge Mountains near Sperryville was "completely cleaned out." The presence of two armies for more than a year had left many acres "almost uncultivated, and no animals are grazing where there used to be hundreds. All fences have been destroyed, and numberless farms burnt, the chimneys alone left standing." Fremantle concluded, "It is difficult to depict and impossible to exaggerate the sufferings which this part of Virginia has undergone." In the fall of 1864, a visitor to Fredericksburg similarly remarked that he saw "not a fence nor an inhabited house" in the surrounding region: "All is still as death for miles and miles under the sweet autumnal sun."[6]

Middle Tennessee presented a comparably bleak picture that mocked its antebellum reputation as an agricultural showplace. The region had been overrun by Federal armies in 1862 and subject to wide-scale foraging for most of the war. "This is a dreary, desolate, barren and deserted looking country," observed a Union officer well before the midpoint of the conflict. "The houses and stores are either closed or smashed to pieces. Everything is going to utter destruction." A northern cavalryman writing in April 1863 anticipated the language Fremantle would use to describe Sperryville two months later: "It is really sad to see this beautiful country here so ruined. There are no fences left at all. There is no corn and hay for the cattle and horses, but there are no horses left anyhow and the planters have no food for themselves." A Confederate passing through the area a few weeks later saw "not a stalk of corn or a blade of wheat growing" and thought "the country wears the most desolate appearance that I have ever seen anywhere."[7]

The valley of the Red River in Louisiana presented an equally dreary picture in mid-1864. Writing to a friend in Texas, Lt. Col. George W. Guess of the 31st Texas Cavalry proclaimed that "not only every vestige of food in the whole country has been destroyed, but nearly every town & every house has been burned." Guess reported that women and children had lost everything "& they are *in the woods* without food, shelter or clothing. There are many that have been in easy circumstances who are actually living on blackberries." None of this came secondhand, affirmed Guest: "These things I know to be true, for I see them with my own eyes. And what a sight!"[8]

Robert Garlick Hill Kean highlighted another dramatic indication of the scope of Confederate defeat. He observed conditions in a number of towns and villages and much of the Virginia back country during a two-week journey in April 1865 and concluded, "The *abolition of slavery* immediately, and by a military order, is the most marked feature of this conquest of the South." Thousands of Confederates doubtless shared Kean's outrage at being forced to reorder southern society without slavery. "Manumission after this fashion will be regarded hereafter," Kean predicted with scarcely controlled anger, "when it has borne its fruits and the passions of the hour have passed away, as the greatest social crime ever committed on the earth." But the North's power was such that white southerners knew they had no option. Kean stated that he "found Virginia quietly submitting to a military government. . . , with small garrisons in all the country towns, the population generally taking the 'amnesty oath,' and all idea of further resistance entirely abandoned."[9]

Abundant testimony of this type could be marshaled to support the point that by the spring of 1865 the Confederacy had absorbed as much punishment as its people could tolerate. Amid increasing deprivation and against mounting odds during the last seven or eight months of fighting, most Confederates had fixed their eyes on Lee and his army to sustain diminishing hopes for independence. The end of the war found them exhausted, unable to muster a satisfactory answer to Sarah Hines's rhetorical "What else could we do but give up." Their shattered landscape, an economic infrastructure in utter disarray, and more than half a million Union soldiers within their borders told them they had been so soundly defeated that further resistance in the name of Confederate nationhood would be chimerical.

Yet as hopes for independence flickered and died, many Confederates expressed continued devotion to their southern nation. Private James A. Scott of the 3rd Virginia Cavalry confessed that he had "much to regret—but it may all be summed up in a word—that I did not do more for my oppressed and unhappy country." Taking comfort from the fact that he had been "able to do even a little" to support the South's fight for independence, Scott insisted that "we were engaged in a just and holy war." He refused to believe so many thousands of Confederates had perished in vain and hoped white southerners would accept their current state of poverty as a challenge to rebuild their troubled land. "We have failed in our efforts to establish a separate nationality," wrote Scott, but "it's hard to think that our glorious old Confederate banner—which we have borne high aloft unconquered so long—must now be furled—but I doubt not—in his own good time God will give us a new & more beautiful one which shall float proudly and wide over all of our foes. Let us put our trust in Him."[10]

A pair of women—one from a prominent slaveholding family and the other from modest working-class circumstances—exemplified civilians whose feelings of Confederate loyalty survived after Appomattox. Elizabeth Pendleton Hardin, a Kentuckian who had lived in various sections of the Confederacy, expressed a "hope I may never again love anything as I loved the cause that is lost." Leaving Eatonton, Georgia, to return to Kentucky in early June 1865, Hardin and her family shouted "Hurrah for Jeff Davis and the Southern Confederacy" as they waved good-bye to their Georgian friends. "We had been there two years and a half, watching with unfaltering hope our struggle for independence and life," wrote Hardin in her diary, "and now that our hopes had all come to naught, we returned to our homes with sad hearts, feeling we had left the brightest part of our lives behind us."[11]

More impressive was the sentiment of a young Richmonder who spoke to John T. Trowbridge in 1865. This woman's father, described by Trowbridge as one of a group of "begrimed laborers" who worked in a nail factory, railed against the Davis government and voiced bitterness that his daughter had been disfigured while working in a laboratory that manufactured ammunition for the Confederate army. The man insisted on showing the northern visitor his daughter's awful wounds, and upon meeting the woman Trowbridge saw that "her hands and face were covered with cruel scars." Quick to offer condolence for her horrible ordeal, Trowbridge was unprepared by her response: "Oh, yes. There was five weeks nobody thought I would live," she said. "But I didn't mind it, for it was for a good cause." When her father responded with "a stream of execrations" against the Confederate government, "the daughter smilingly repeated, 'It was a good cause, and I don't regret it. You musn't mind what he says.'" Unable to fathom the young woman's loyalty to the dead Confederacy, Trowbridge doubted her sanity.[12] Historians who insist that class conflict deeply divided the Confederate populace likely would join Trowbridge in wondering why a working-class woman who so obviously should have been disaffected was not.

Few former Confederates believed the war had proved secession illegal. Armed might alone, rather than constitutional authority, lay behind the North's ability to label former Confederates as traitors. Two witnesses elaborated common themes. John Richard Dennett, who traveled the immediate postwar South as a correspondent for the *Nation,* talked with a man in Richmond who proclaimed that the "people of the South feel that they have been most unjustly, most tyrannically oppressed by the North. All our rights have been trampled upon." Although Confederates had been "subjugated, conquered, and in their collective capacity they must submit to whatever may be inflicted upon them," this man averred that they "had a most perfect right to secede, and we have been slaughtered by the thousands for attempting to exercise it." He added darkly that "the people of the South are not going to stand that." A Unionist judge from Alexandria, Virginia, pointed to similar sentiment among ex-Confederates. "They boast of their treason," he told the Joint Committee on Reconstruction in January 1866, "and ten or eleven out of the twelve on any jury . . . would say that Lee was almost equal to Washington, and was the noblest man in the State, and they regard every man who has committed treason with more favor than any man in the State who has remained loyal to the government." A member of the Committee asked if the judge referred to people across the entire state of Virginia. "Yes, sir," came the reply.[13]

White southerners who retained Confederate loyalties typically harbored deep resentments against Federal soldiers and northerners in general. Although compelled to acknowledge Union success in suppressing their struggle for independence, Confederates defiantly refused to forgive enemies who had inflicted such pain on their society. Elizabeth Hardin and Anne S. Frobel used their diaries to vent hatred for Yankees shared by untold others. "The Psalmist and I are alike in one respect at least," remarked Hardin in a passage rich in biblical allusions. "We both have seen the wicked flourish like a green bay tree and the vilest men exalted." Hardin wished the French would make trouble for the United States in Mexico: "I would like to cry, 'Vive la France!' I am afraid I would be tempted to cry 'Vive Beelzebub' if he were fighting the Yankees."[14]

Frobel's animosity toward Yankees was such that she believed they arranged accidents to kill Confederate prisoners of war attempting to return south. "I cannot under stand how it is that so many Confederate prisoners being sent home are lost," she wrote in frustration and anger. "In every paper we see now there is some terrible account of disaster to Confederates[.] [A]t one place a boat was snagged and two, or three, hundred drowned. Then a train ran off the track, and a great number killed[.] The last account was of a boat load, between Ft Lookout and Savanna being scalded to death by the steams being turned on them (accidentally of course)[.]" More immediately, Union soldiers stationed near Frobel's farm in Fairfax County, Virginia, during the summer of 1865 pulled down fences, drank her well dry, commandeered her stables for their mounts, and generally disrupted her life. "There is no annoyance conceivable that these dreadful people do not inflict on us," she complained. After Union soldiers swarmed around her well and left the water "entirely unfit for use" during a July 4th celebration, Frobel lashed out against the "selfish—miserable wretches" who had acted, she stressed, in typical Yankee fashion.[15]

Northern soldiers frequently commented about the insolence and animosity they perceived among former Confederates. One such ob-server was Union sergeant Mathew Woodruff, who betrayed reciprocal dislike for white southerners in relating an incident in Mobile, Alabama. When a black woman reprimanded three young girls for waving a rebel flag, the children's mother "appeared with a saucy rebuke & insults to all *Yanks,* saying 'they' (the south was not whiped) & if they got a chance would rise again." Woodruff believed these "to be the prevail-ing sentiments throughout the South." He added, "There is not 9 out of 10 of these so called 'Whiped' traitors that I would trust until I saw the rope applied to their Necks, then I would only have Faith in the quality of the rope."[16]

Sergeant Woodruff would have said that the song "O, I'm a Good Old Rebel"—the 1866 sheet music for which was sarcastically dedicated to "the Hon. Thad. Stevens"—accurately reflected widespread feelings among ex-Confederates. Its bitter lyrics combined pride in the Confederacy, recognition that further armed resistance was impossible, and determination to keep alive hatred for the northern foe:

> Three hundred thousand Yankees is stiff in Southern dust.
> We got three hundred thousand before they conquered us.
> They died of Southern fever and Southern steel and shot,
> I wish they was three million instead of what we got.
>
> I can't take up my musket and fight them now no more,
> But I ain't gonna love them, now that is certain sure.
> And I don't want no pardon for what I was and am.
> I won't be reconstructed, and I don't care a damn.[17]

Former Confederate corps commander Jubal A. Early represented in flesh and blood this song's unrepentant rebel. A leading architect of Lost Cause explanations for the coming of the war and the reasons for Confederate defeat, he labored indefatigably to create a written record of the conflict favorable to the Confederacy.[18] Two letters from Robert E. Lee, who cared deeply about how future generations would understand the war, helped galvanize Early. In November 1865, Lee informed Early that he intended to write a history of the Army of Northern Virginia that would "transmit, if possible, the truth to posterity, and do justice to our brave soldiers." Four months later Lee asked Early for any information he had relating to "numbers, destruction of private property by the Federal troops, &c." during 1864 and 1865. Lee hoped to demonstrate the discrepancy in strength between Union and Confederate forces, though he believed it would "be difficult to get the world to understand the odds against which we fought." Predicting that former Confederates would have to endure false accounts of their actions and circumstances, Lee averred that they must "be patient, & suffer for awhile at least" because "at present the public mind is not prepared to receive the truth." Early later urged Lee to complete his history of the Confederate army in Virginia, affirming that a written record of the war was crucial. "The most that is left to us is the history of our struggle," he stated, "and I think that ought to be accurately written. We lost nearly everything but honor, and that should be religiously guarded."[19]

In a landmark Lost Cause speech delivered on the anniversary of Lee's death in 1872, Early stressed themes he and his old chief had raised in their correspondence. Much of the address focused on the over-whelming power of the North. Early brilliantly cast Lee and his gallant soldiers against a mechanistic Federal juggernaut: "General Lee had not been conquered in battle, but surrendered because he had no longer an army with which to give battle. What he surrendered was the skeleton, the mere ghost of the Army of Northern Virginia, which had been gradually worn down by the combined agencies of numbers, steam-power, railroads, mechanism, and all the resources of physical science." Years of Federal strategic offensives, fueled by unlimited manpower and material wealth, "had finally produced that exhaustion of our army and resources, and that accumulation of numbers on the other side, which wrought the final disaster."

Early implored his audience not to turn their backs "on the graves of our fallen heroes" and to "cherish the remembrance of their deeds, and see that justice is done to their memories." The Confederate experiment had been a noble attempt to protect southern principles, and Early charged veterans to hold dear "the holy memories connected with our glorious though unsuccessful struggle." Turning to the women in attendance, he expressed confidence that they would "continue to honor the brave dead, and strew flowers on their graves." It would be their duty "to instil the sentiments of honor and patriotism into the hearts of the rising and future generations, and teach them to venerate the memory, emulate the virtues and cherish the principles of those who fell fighting for your homes, your all."

Early saw Lee as central to the process of remembering and honoring the Confederacy—just as the Confederate people had seen him as central to their hopes for independence. "It is a vain work for us to seek anywhere for a parallel to the great character which has won our admiration and love," Early insisted. "Our beloved Chief stands, like some lofty column which rears its head among the highest, in grandeur, simple, pure and sublime, needing no borrowed lustre; and he is all our own." The South should "see that a monument to his glorious memory is erected at the Confederate Capital, in defence of which his wondrous talents and sublime virtues were displayed." Future visitors to the site would know that Lee's soldiers had "remained true to him in death, and were not unworthy to have been the followers of ROBERT E. LEE."[20]

Most former Confederates readily embraced the major elements of Early's address—all of which were repeated endlessly by other southern lecturers and writers during the postwar years. The emphasis on northern advantages of men and resources, the righteousness of the Confederates' own motives, and Lee's greatness resonated powerfully among a people who had sacrificed so much in a failed war. Defeat following a supreme effort against long odds entailed no loss of honor, and the example of Lee as an ideal Christian warrior provided a hero worthy of placement alongside George Washington.

Frustrated in their attempt to found a new slaveholding republic, former Confederates replaced wartime national purpose with postwar determination to keep alive the memory of their struggle. Ladies' associations spearheaded efforts to gather the Confederate dead in special sections of cemeteries, where long rows of uniform white headstones recalled the war's human cost. Crowds gathered annually in those places to decorate Confederate graves and hear addresses about the courage and steadfastness of the honored dead. Scores of monuments to commemorate leading military and political figures, as well as the common soldiers and women of the Confederacy, went up on courthouse grounds, in cemeteries, and on battlefields. The birthdays of Jefferson Davis and Robert E. Lee became state holidays. Speeches at the dedication of monuments, on holidays associated with the war, and at reunions of veterans reminded white southerners of their four-year ordeal, as did prints depicting heroes and wartime events that graced the walls of their homes. In these and other ways the memory of the Confederacy lived on with the generation that fought the war.[21]

Time inevitably banked the passions that had animated white southerners during the war and in the early postbellum years. Virtually all former Confederates eventually accepted at least some degree of reconciliation with the North. But that realistic accommodation should not obscure the depth of their commitment to the Confederacy. They fought doggedly to create a new slaveholding republic and, with Lee and his army as their military centerpiece, more than once nearly broke northern resolve. Persevering despite great adversity, they surrendered only when their pool of manpower had been ravaged, Union armies stood poised to smash opposing Confederate forces, and much of their country literally lay in ruins. After Appomattox, they sullenly conceded the superiority of northern power but insisted that they had fought for a worthy cause.

It defies modern understanding that any people—especially one in which nonslaveholding yeomen formed a solid majority—would pour energy and resources into a fight profoundly tainted by the institution of slavery. Yet the Confederate people did so. Until historians can explain more fully why they did, the story of the Civil War will remain woefully incomplete.

Notes

Index

NOTES

....

Abbreviations

B&L	Robert Underwood Johnson and Clarence Clough Buel, eds., *Battles and Leaders of the Civil War,* 4 vols. (New York: Century, 1887)
FSNMP	Fredericksburg and Spotsylvania National Military Park Library, Fredericksburg, Virginia
OR	U.S. War Department, *The War of the Rebellion: A Compilation of the Official Records of the Union and Confederate Armies,* 127 vols., index, and atlas (Washington, D.C.: GPO, 1880–1901)
SHC	Southern Historical Collection, Wilson Library, University of North Carolina, Chapel Hill
VHS	Virginia Historical Society, Richmond

Introduction

1. James M. McPherson has stressed that "there was nothing inevitable about northern victory in the Civil War." Success depended on maintaining national morale, and morale in turn was tied to military campaigns. "There were several major turning points," argued McPherson in "American Victory, American Defeat" (in Gabor S. Boritt, ed., *Why the Confederacy Lost* [New York: Oxford University Press, 1992]), pp. 40–41, "points of contingency when events moved in one direction but could well have moved in another." Among these points were George B. McClellan's failure to capture Richmond in July 1862, the Confederate strategic offensives in the fall of 1862, Robert E. Lee's invasion of

Pennsylvania in the summer of 1863, and William T. Sherman's capture of Atlanta in September 1864.

2. Robert Penn Warren, *Jefferson Davis Gets His Citizenship Back* (Lexington: University Press of Kentucky, 1980), pp. 58–59.

3. Geoffrey C. Ward and others, *The Civil War: An Illustrated History* (New York: Alfred A. Knopf, 1990), p. 272. Burns took a similar position in his television documentary *The Civil War*. For a discussion of Burns's documentary treatment, see Gary W. Gallagher, "How Familiarity Bred Success: Military Campaigns and Leaders in Ken Burns's *The Civil War*," in Robert Brent Toplin, ed., *Ken Burns's "The Civil War": Historians Respond* (New York: Oxford University Press, 1996), pp. 43–45.

4. Lucy W. Otey to Colonel Lyle Charles, March 8, 1864, quoted in Sword & Saber, *Holiday Catalogue 1995* (Gettysburg, Pa.: Sword & Saber, 1995), pp. 9–10; [Anna Maria Green], *The Journal of a Milledgeville Girl, 1861–1867,* ed. James C. Bonner, University of Georgia Libraries, Miscellanea Publications no. 4 (Athens: University of Georgia Press, 1964), p. 63 (entry for November 25, 1864).

5. Frank Goodrow to Mr. Banks, June 4, 1864, quoted in Sword & Saber, *Catalogue 74: Fall of 1994* (Gettysburg, Pa.: Sword & Saber, 1994), p. 20; Luther Rice Mills to John Mills, June 6, 1864, in George D. Harmon, ed., "Letters of Luther Rice Mills—A Confederate Soldier," *North Carolina Historical Review* 4 (July 1927): 300–301.

6. Rufus A. Barrier to "Dear Father," March 6, 1864, in Rufus Alexander Barrier and William Lafayette Barrier, *Dear Father: Confederate Letters Never Before Published,* ed. Beverly Barrier Troxler and Billy Dawn Barrier Auciello (North Billerica, Mass.: Autumn Printing, 1989), p. 41; Daniel Pope to his wife, March 12, 1864, in Mills Lane, ed., *"Dear Mother: Don't grieve about me. If I get killed, I'll only be dead": Letters from Georgia Soldiers in the Civil War* (Savannah, Ga.: Beehive Press, 1977), pp. 282–283.

7. *Testimony of James B. Gardner, Deputy Executive Director American Historical Association, Before the Subcommittee on National Parks and Public Lands, Committee on Interior and Insular Affairs of the U.S. House of Representatives, H.R. 3513 and S. 1770, September 4, 1990* (Washington, D.C.: American Historical Association, 1990), pp. 2–3. On attitudes among academic historians toward the military side of the Civil War, see James M. McPherson, "What's the Matter with History?" in McPherson, *Drawn with the Sword: Reflections on the American Civil War* (New York: Oxford University Press, 1996), especially pp. 240–242.

McPherson also addresses the phenomenon of Civil War buffs seemingly uninterested in anything but battles and generals.

8. Macon (Georgia) *Journal and Messenger,* July 1, 1863; Edward A. O'Neal, Jr., to George M. Peek, Peek Family Papers, SHC; Abraham Lincoln, "Second Inaugural Address," in Abraham Lincoln, *The Collected Works of Abraham Lincoln,* ed. Roy P. Basler, 9 vols. (New Brunswick, N.J.: Rutgers University Press, 1953), vol. 8, p. 332.

9. E. C. Boudinot to W. P. Boudinot, June 2, 1864, in Edward Everett Dale and Gaston Litton, eds., *Cherokee Cavaliers: Forty Years of Cherokee History as Told in the Correspondence of the Ridge-Watie-Boudinot Family* (Norman: University of Oklahoma Press, 1939), p. 170.

10. Thomas Bailey to T. J. McKie, July 11, 1864, quoted in Sword & Saber, *Catalogue 65: Fall of 1992* (Gettysburg, Pa.: Sword & Saber, 1992), p. 31.

1. Popular Will

1. Eric Foner, "Slavery, the War, and Reconstruction," in Eric Foner, ed., *The New American History* (Philadelphia: Temple University Press, 1990), pp. 81–82. In *What They Fought For, 1861–1865* (Baton Rouge: Louisiana State University Press, 1994), p. 15, James M. McPherson noted: "I found less evidence of the 'rich man's war/poor man's fight' attitude in soldiers' letters than I expected, given the prevalence of this theme in recent scholarship." McPherson based his conclusions on the letters and diaries of 374 Confederate soldiers, about two-thirds of whom were slaveholders.

2. Bell I. Wiley, *The Road to Appomattox* (Memphis: Memphis State College Press, 1956), p. 78; E. Merton Coulter, *The Confederate States of America, 1861–1865* (Baton Rouge: Louisiana State University Press, 1950), pp. 566–567; Richard E. Beringer, Herman Hattaway, Archer Jones, and William N. Still, Jr., *Why the South Lost the Civil War* (Athens: University of Georgia Press, 1986), p. 64. James M. McPherson has observed that "if one analyzes carefully the lack-of-will thesis as it is spelled out in several studies, it becomes clear that what the authors are really writing about is loss of the will to carry on, not an initial *lack* of will. The book *Why the South Lost the Civil War,* which builds its interpretation around the *lack*-of-will thesis, abounds with *loss*-of-will phraseology." James M. McPherson, "American Victory, American Defeat," in Gabor S. Boritt, ed., *Why the Confederacy Lost* (New York: Oxford University Press, 1992), p. 34.

3. Charles Grier Sellers, Jr., "The Travail of Slavery," in Charles Grier Sellers, Jr., ed., *The Southerner as American* (Chapel Hill: University of North Carolina Press, 1960), pp. 70–71; Wiley, *Road to Appomattox,* pp. 120–121.

4. Malcolm C. McMillan, *The Disintegration of a Confederate State: Three Governors and Alabama's Home Front, 1861–1865* (Macon, Ga.: Mercer University Press, 1986), p. 127; Steven Hahn, *The Roots of Southern Populism: Yeoman Farmers and the Transformation of the Georgia Upcountry, 1850–1890* (New York: Oxford University Press, 1983), p. 132; Paul D. Escott, *After Secession: Jefferson Davis and the Failure of Confederate Nationalism* (Baton Rouge: Louisiana State University Press, 1978), pp. 126, 197; Wiley, *Road to Appomattox,* p. 67. Seemingly content to end his examination in the aftermath of Gettysburg and Vicksburg and let his generalizations stand without significant support, Hahn did not explore in any depth conditions and attitudes in Georgia after the summer of 1863.

5. Fred Arthur Bailey, *Class and Tennessee's Confederate Generation* (Chapel Hill: University of North Carolina Press, 1987), pp. 86, 104; Reid Mitchell, "The Creation of Confederate Loyalties," in Robert H. Abzug and Stephen E. Maizlich, eds., *New Perspectives on Race and Slavery in America: Essays in Honor of Kenneth M. Stampp* (Lexington: University Press of Kentucky, 1986), p. 97. In contrast to the prevailing picture, Stephen V. Ash's pioneering study of the occupied Confederacy discovered relatively little class warfare: "Of all the struggles that convulsed the occupied South—including those of Rebels versus Yankees, secessionists versus Unionists, and whites versus blacks—the struggle of the propertied versus the propertyless was the most retsrained. Dead bodies of insurgent poor whites did not litter the countryside as the bodies of insurgent blacks and Unionists and invading Yankees did." Stephen V. Ash, *When the Yankees Came: Conflict and Chaos in the Occupied South, 1861–1865* (Chapel Hill: University of North Carolina Press, 1995), p. 193.

6. Escott, *After Secession,* xi; Lawrence N. Powell and Michael S. Wayne, "Self Interest and the Decline of Confederate Nationalism," in Harry P. Owen and James J. Cooke, eds., *The Old South in the Crucible of War* (Jackson: University Press of Mississippi, 1983), p. 30.

7. Wayne K. Durrill, *War of Another Kind: A Southern Community in the Great Rebellion* (New York: Oxford University Press, 1990), pp. 37, 241. Durrill's heavy-handed materialist explanations for behavior ignore a mass of written evidence suggesting far more complex motives. The relative dearth of letters and diaries from the yeomanry makes it easier to generalize about them without fear of contradiction from their own testimony.

8. Elizabeth Fox-Genovese and Eugene D. Genovese, *Fruits of Merchant Capital: Slavery and Bourgeois Property in the Rise and Expansion of Capitalism* (New York: Oxford University Press, 1983), pp. 256–257. Hahn drew a distinction between upcountry and other yeomen but also generalized about all Confederate yeomen.

9. Drew Gilpin Faust, *Mothers of Invention: Women of the Slaveholding South in the American Civil War* (Chapel Hill: University of North Carolina Press, 1996), pp. 238, 247; Drew Gilpin Faust, "Altars of Sacrifice: Confederate Women and the Narratives of War," *Journal of American History* 76 (March 1990): 1228; George C. Rable, *Civil Wars: Women and the Crisis of Southern Nationalism* (Urbana: University of Illinois Press, 1989), pp. 211–213. LeeAnn Whites, in *The Civil War as a Crisis in Gender: Augusta, Georgia, 1860–1890* (Athens: University of Georgia Press, 1995), highlighted tensions between wealthy and poorer white women as the war threw more women of all classes into the public sphere. "As less privileged white women in the city began to assert publicly the legitimacy of their own domestic position," asserted Whites, "more elite Confederate women began to realize that public empowerment for all white women could also entail a loss for their own class" (p. 13).

10. Beringer and others, *Why the South Lost,* p. 427.

11. Wiley, *Road to Appomattox,* 104–105; Sellers, "Travail of Slavery," pp. 51–52.

12. Kenneth M. Stampp, "The Southern Road to Appomattox," in Kenneth M. Stampp, *The Imperiled Union: Essays on the Background of the Civil War* (New York: Oxford University Press, 1980), pp. 260, 264–267. It seems almost too obvious to mention that many thousands of Confederates "accepted the abolition of slavery" only because Federal armies triumphed on the battlefield. Southern white determination to restore black people to a condition as close to servitude as possible over the next several decades suggests that they lamented rather than welcomed the loss of slavery.

13. Beringer and others, *Why the South Lost,* pp. 439–440, 425–426.

14. Ibid., p. 442; Hahn, *Roots of Southern Populism,* pp. 132–133. Hahn unpersuasively attempted to place yeoman sacrifice within his class framework: "Yet, the very perseverance of these small farmers may have expressed distinctive class feelings in no less compelling a way than did the desertions of many of their counterparts . . . They fought for a 'liberty and independence' not beholden to slaveownership but rooted in communities of petty producers."

15. For Confederate and Union strengths and losses, see E. B. Long, *The Civil War Day by Day: An Almanac, 1861–1865* (Garden City, N.Y.: Doubleday, 1971), pp. 710–711; Herman Hattaway and Archer Jones, *How the North Won: A Military History of the Civil War* (Urbana: University of Illinois Press, 1983), pp. 115–116; and James M. McPherson, *Ordeal by Fire: The Civil War and Reconstruction,* rev. ed. (New York: McGraw-Hill, 1992), p. 184. The 1860 census placed at 1,064,193 the number of white males between the ages of 18 and 45 in the eleven Confederate states. Joseph C. G. Kennedy, comp., *Population of the United States in 1860; Compiled from the Original returns of the Eighth Census, Under the Direction of the Secretary of the Interior* (Washington, D.C.: GPO, 1864), p. xvii. It is possible that the Confederacy mustered as many as 900,000 of its military-age white population, but such a figure cannot be supported with any certainty. Further research in materials at the National Archives may permit a more definitive calculation of how many men entered Confderate service.

16. Long, *Civil War Day by Day,* pp. 711–712; U.S. Department of Commerce, *Historical Statistics of the United States: Colonial Times to the Present,* 2 vols. (Washington, D.C.: Bureau of the Census, 1975), vol. 2, p. 1135; Allan R. Millett and Peter Maslowski, *For the Common Defense: A Military History of the United States of America* (New York: The Free Press, 1984), p. 542. If compared to the populations of their societies as a whole, the Vietnam casualties drop considerably farther behind those of the Confederacy (even with slave population added to the Confederate total).

17. These figures are from McPherson, *Ordeal by Fire,* p. 475.

18. On Pennsylvania and the Confederate invasion, see William A. Blair, "'A Source of Amusement': Pennsylvania Versus Lee, 1863," *Pennsylvania Magazine of History and Biography* 105 (July 1991): 319–338. Blair mentioned widespread unhappiness with the central government because of conscription and a heated gubernatorial race as factors that vitiated Governor Andrew Gregg Curtin's effort to rally Pennsylvanians to defend their state. "Civilian response to the emergency," noted Blair, "earned the state the scorn of many northerners" (p. 320). In June and July 1863, many soldiers in both the Army of the Potomac and the Army of Northern Virginia described a lack of Union patriotism among the civilians of southern Pennsylvania. On this phenomenon, see Edwin B. Coddington, *The Gettysburg Campaign: A Study in Command* (New York: Charles Scribner's Sons, 1968), pp. 140–143.

19. Abraham Lincoln, memorandum concerning his probable re-election, August 23,

1864, in Abraham Lincoln, *The Collected Works of Abraham Lincoln,* ed. Roy P. Basler, 9 vols. (New Brunswick, N.J.: Rutgers University Press, 1953), vol. 7, p. 514; Ella Lonn, *Desertion during the Civil War* (New York: Century, 1928), pp. 205–206; Robert E. Sterling, "Civil War Draft Resistance in the Middle West," 2 vols. (Ph.D. diss., University of Northern Illinois, 1974), vol. 1, pp. 273–274.

20. William Dickey to his wife, July 13, 1864, in Mills Lane, ed., *"Dear Mother: Don't grieve about me. If I get killed, I'll only be dead": Letters from Georgia Soldiers in the Civil War* (Savannah, Ga.: Beehive Press, 1977), p. 315; Lonn, *Desertion during the Civil War,* pp. 231–232. As stern a general as Jubal A. Early recognized that there were different types of deserters: "Now God forbid that I should say one word in justification of desertion under any circumstances," he wrote in 1866. "I had no toleration for it during the war, and never failed to sanction and order the execution of sentences for the extreme penalty for that offence, when submitted to me; but some palliation was to be found for the conduct of many of those who did desert, in the fact that they did so to go to the aid of their families, who they knew were suffering for the necessaries of life . . ." Jubal A. Early, *A Memoir of the Last Year of the War for Independence, in the Confederate States of America* (Toronto: Lovell & Gibson, 1866), pp. 127–128.

21. William A. Blair, ""Virginia's Private War: The Contours of Dissent and Loyalty in the Confederacy, 1861–1865 (Ph.D. diss., Pennsylvania State University, 1995), pp. 103–104; Kevin Conley Ruffner, "Civil War Desertion from a Black Belt Regiment: An Examination of the 44th Virginia Infantry," in Edward L. Ayers and John C. Willis, eds., *The Edge of the South: Life in Nineteenth-Century Virginia* (Charlottesville: University Press of Virginia, 1991), p. 100; William E. Emerson, "Leadership and Civil War Desertion in the Twenty-fourth and Twenty-fifth Regiments North Carolina Troops," *Southern Historian* 17 (Spring 1996): 27–29.

22. Henry Butler to Capt. William Paisley, March 10, 1865, in Elizabeth Paisley Huckaby and Ethel C. Simpson, eds., *Tulip Evermore: Emma Butler and William Paisley, Their Lives and Letters, 1857–1887* (Fayetteville: University of Arkansas Press, 1985), p. 57.

23. Reid Mitchell, "The Perseverance of the Soldiers," in Boritt, *Why the Confederacy Lost,* pp. 111, 124; Wiley, *Road to Appomattox,* pp. 119–121.

24. These strengths are taken from Ernest B. Furgurson, *Chancellorsville 1863: The Souls of the Brave* (New York: Knopf, 1992), p. 88; Gordon C. Rhea, *The Battle of the Wilderness:*

May 5–6, 1864 (Baton Rouge: Louisiana State University Press, 1994), p. 21; Chris M. Calkins, *The Final Bivouac: The Surrender Parade at Appomattox and the Disbanding of the Armies, April 10–May 20, 1865* (Lynchburg, Va.: H. E. Howard, 1988), pp. 204–208.

25. John Preston to James A. Seddon, April 30, 1864, in *OR*, ser. 4, vol. 3, pp. 354–364. Additional research may reveal why the draft was more successful in some Confederate states than in others. Population density, attitudes among local officials, and other factors likely played a role.

26. John Ott to Maria C. Massie, October 8, 1864, in Oliver Morris Refsell, "The Massies of Virginia: Documentary History of a Planter Family," 2 vols. (Ph.D. diss., University of Texas, 1959), vol. 2, pp. 1109–1110.

27. Jonathan M. Bryant, *How Curious a Land: Conflict and Change in Greene County, Georgia, 1850–1885* (Chapel Hill: University of North Carolina Press, 1996), pp. 84–85.

28. Edward A. Pollard, *Southern History of the War: The Last Year of the War* (New York: Charles B. Richardson, 1866), pp. 13–14. On Confederate expectations in the spring of 1864, see Gary W. Gallagher, "'Our Hearts Are Full of Hope': The Army of Northern Virginia in the Spring of 1864," in Gallagher, ed., *The Wilderness Campaign* (Chapel Hill: University of North Carolina Press, 1997).

29. Atlanta *Southern Confederacy,* March 24, 1864; Richmond *Dispatch,* March 1, 1864; Richmond *Enquirer,* February 6, 1864; Charleston *Daily Courier,* February 26, 1864. The piece in the *Southern Confederacy* was clipped from the Mobile *Advertiser.*

30. Charles Minnigerode to "My Dearest Mother," April 26, 1864, typescript in collections of Richmond National Battlefield Park Library, Richmond, Virginia; Reuben Allen Pierson to William H. Pierson, March 22, 1864, Pierson Family Papers, Tulane University, New Orleans, La.; George W. Ingram to his wife, April 16, 1864, in Charles R. Schultz, ed., *Hurrah for the Texans: Civil War Letters of George W. Ingram* (College Station: Texas A&M University Library, 1974), p. 23; A. J. Neal to his sister, March 23, 1864, in Lane, *Dear Mother,* p. 285.

31. John B. Jones, *A Rebel War Clerk's Diary at the Confederate States Capital,* 2 vols. (1866; reprint, Alexandria, Va.: Time-Life Books, 1982), vol. 2, pp. 195–196; Robert Garlick Hill Kean, *Inside the Confederate Government: The Diary of Robert Garlick Hill Kean,* ed. Edward Younger (New York: Oxford University Press, 1957), pp. 143–144 (entry for April 3, 1864); Mary Jones to Mary S. Mallard, April 30, 1864, in Robert Manson Myers,

ed., *The Children of Pride: A True Story of Georgia and the Civil War* (New Haven, Conn.: Yale University Press, 1972), pp. 1162–1163.

32. James Keith to Juliet (Chilton) Keith, November 16, 1864, Keith Family Papers, VHS; Wiley J. Smith to Nannie Smith, January 23, 1865, Wiley J. Smith Letters, Drawer 171, Box 7 (microfilm), Georgia State Archives, Atlanta.

33. Letter of "J. W. G." dated November 17, 1864, published in the Columbus (Ga.) *Daily Enquirer,* November 26, 1864. In contrast to soldiers in the Army of Tennessee during operations in November and December 1864, Confederates opposing Sherman's march from Atlanta to Savannah—a high proportion of whom were calvalrymen—exhibited relatively poor morale. On this point, see Joseph T. Glatthaar, *The March to the Sea and Beyond: Sherman's Troops in the Savannah and Carolinas Campaigns* (New York: New York University Press, 1985), pp. 162–163.

34. David Golightly Harris, *Piedmont Farmer: The Journals of David Golightly Harris, 1855–1870,* ed. Philip N. Racine (Knoxville: University of Tennessee Press, 1990), p. 349 (entry for November 8, 1864); Francis W. Dawson to "My Dear Mother," November 25, 1864, printed in Francis W. Dawson, *Reminiscences of a Confederate Soldier* (1882; reprint, Baton Rouge: Louisiana State University Press, 1980), p. 204.

35. William M. Baines to George Washington Baines, February 8, 1865, Papers of Rebekah Baines Johnson, Lyndon Baines Johnson Library, Austin, Texas; Sallie Bird to Saida Bird, February 5, 1865, in John Rozier, ed., *The Granite Farm Letters: The Civil War Correspondence of Edgeworth & Sallie Bird* (Athens: University of Georgia Press, 1988), pp. 243–244.

36. John Wood to his father, December 17, 1864, in Lane, *Dear Mother,* p. 338; Susan Emiline Jeffords Caldwell to Lycurgus Washington Caldwell, March 26, 1865, in J. Michael Walton, ed., *"My Heart is So Rebellious": The Caldwell Letters, 1861–1865* (Warrenton, Va.: Fauquier National Bank, n.d. [circa 1992]), pp. 261–262; Jared E. Stalling to his wife, March 5, 1865, Jared E. Stalling Papers, Special Collections, Texas Christian University, Fort Worth.

37. Tully Francis Parker to his wife and children, May 4, 1864, typescript in bound vol. 201, FSNMP; Abram Hayne Young to "Dear Parents and Sisters," March 13, 1864, in Mary Wyche Burgess, ed., "Civil War Letters of Abram Hayne Young," *South Carolina Historical Magazine* 78 (January 1977): 63.

....

38. Kate Cumming, *The Journal of a Confederate Nurse,* ed. Richard B. Harwell (Savannah, Ga.: Beehive Press, 1975), pp. 229–230 (entry for December 25, 1864); Emma Holmes, *The Diary of Miss Emma Holmes, 1861–1866,* ed. John F. Marszalek (Baton Rouge: Louisiana State University Press, 1979), pp. 436–437.

39. Stampp, "The Southern Road to Appomattox," pp. 260, 267; Wiley, *Road to Appomattox,* pp. 104–105. Stampp omitted the crucial first sentence of this passage from Porcher's letter.

40. R. E. Lee to Andrew Hunter, January 11, 1865, in *OR,* ser. 4, vol. 3, pp. 1012–1013; William Allan, "Memoranda of Conversations with General Robert E. Lee," in Gary W. Gallagher, ed., *Lee the Soldier* (Lincoln: University of Nebraska Press, 1996), p. 12. Lee also broached the topic with William Preston Johnston, the son of Confederate general Albert Sidney Johnston, in 1868. Johnston recorded that Lee "claimed that he knew the strength of the United States Government; and saw the necessity at first of two things—a proclamation of gradual emancipation and the use of negroes as soldiers, and second the necessity of the early and prompt exportation of the cotton." William Preston Johnston, "Memoranda of Conversations with General R. E. Lee," in Gallagher, ed., *Lee the Soldier,* pp. 29–30.

41. Clarence L. Mohr, *On the Threshold of Freedom: Masters and Slaves in Civil War Georgia* (Athens: University of Georgia Press, 1986), p. 265; John Cimprich, *Slavery's End in Tennessee, 1861–1865* (University: University of Alabama Press, 1985), p. 4; Ash, *When the Yankees Came,* pp. 153, 168–169.

42. Mary Chesnut, *Mary Chesnut's Civil War,* ed. C. Vann Woodward (New Haven, Conn.: Yale University Press, 1981), p. 29; Elizabeth Fox-Genovese, *Within the Plantation Household: Black and White Women of the Old South* (Chapel Hill: University of North Carolina Press, 1988), p. 334; Fox-Genovese, *To Be Worthy of God's Favor: Southern Women's Defense and Critique of Slavery,* 32nd annual Robert Fortenbaugh Memorial Lecture (Gettysburg, Pa.: Gettysburg College, 1993), p. 7.

43. Eliza Francis Andrews, *The War-Time Journal of a Georgia Girl, 1864–1865,* ed. Spencer Birdwell King, Jr. (1908; reprint, Atlanta: Cherokee Publishing, 1976), pp. 69, 127 (entries for January 15, April 1, 1865); Catherine Ann Devereux Edmondston, *"Journal of a Secesh Lady": The Diary of Catherine Ann Devereux Edmondston, 1860–1866,* ed. Beth Gilbert Crabtree and James W. Patton (Raleigh: North Carolina Division of Archives and History, 1979), p. 651 (entry for December 30, 1864). On Confederate sentiment in favor

of making bondage less oppressive for the slaves, see Mohr, *On the Threshold of Freedom,* especially Chapter 8.

44. Mary Jane Fulton to Pembroke Thom, January 24, 1864, in Catherine Thom Bartlett, ed., *"My Dear Brother": A Confederate Chronicle* (Richmond, Va.: Dietz Press, 1952), p. 145; William Lyne Wilson to "My Dearest Mother," April 19, 1864, in Festus P. Summers, ed., *A Borderland Confederate* (Pittsburgh: University of Pittsburgh Press, 1962), p. 78; Thomas J. Goree to Sarah Williams Kittrell Goree, April 26, 1864, in Thomas J. Goree, *Longstreet's Aide: The Civil War Letters of Major Thomas J. Goree,* ed. Thomas W. Cutrer (Charlottesville: University Press of Virginia, 1995), pp. 122–123.

45. Peter S. Carmichael, *Lee's Young Artillerist: William R. J. Pegram* (Charlottesville: University Press of Virginia, 1995), pp. 5, 157; Stephen Dodson Ramseur to David Schenck, October 10, 1864, Stephen Dodson Ramseur Papers, SHC. For a valuable discussion of religion as a motivating factor among Confederate soldiers, see Samuel J. Watson, "Religion and Combat Motivation in the Confederate Armies," *Journal of Military History* 58 (January 1994): 29–55. Watson concluded, "Religious belief permeated the entire matrix of Confederate combat motivation. Faith was intimately connected with the national cause at all levels and times, from enlistment to the aftermath of battle" (p. 55).

46. F. Stanley Russell to "Dear Papa," March 14, 1864, in F. Stanley Russell, *The Letters of F. Stanley Russell: The Movements of Company H, Thirteenth Virginia Regiment, Confederate States Army 1861–1864,* ed. Douglas Carroll (Baltimore: Paul M. Harrod Co., 1963), p. 62; Ted Barclay to "Dear Sister," May 2, 1864, in Ted Barclay, *Ted Barclay, Liberty Hall Volunteers: Letters from the Stonewall Brigade (1861–1864),* ed. Charles W. Turner (Natural Bridge Station, Va.: Rockbridge Publishing Co., 1992), pp. 143–144.

47. Samuel C. Clyde to Hattie Crook, April 28, 1864, typescript in the collections of FSNMP.

48. Gardiner H. Shattuck, Jr., *A Shield and Hiding Place: The Religious Life of the Civil War Armies* (Macon, Ga.: Mercer University Press, 1987), pp. 102–108; George Cary Eggleston, *A Rebel's Recollections,* ed. David Donald (1875; reprint, Bloomington: Indiana University Press, 1959), pp. 176–177; Thomas Conolly, *An Irishman in Dixie: Thomas Conolly's Diary of the Fall of the Confederacy,* ed. Nelson D. Lankford (Columbia: University of South Carolina Press, 1988), p. 83; Sarah Morgan, *The Civil War Diary of Sarah Morgan,* ed. Charles East (Athens: University of Georgia Press, 1991), p. 606.

....

49. Charles S. Wainwright, *A Diary of Battle: The Personal Journals of Colonel Charles S. Wainwright, 1861–1865,* ed. Allan Nevins (New York: Harcourt, Brace & World, 1962), pp. 520–521.

50. Fox-Genovese and Genovese, *Fruits of Merchant Capital,* p. 264.

51. Correspondent A. Le Francois in *Le Temps,* September 10, 1864. Donald E. Witt of Winchester, Virginia, a scholar of French literature with a deep interest in the American Civil War, kindly made available his translations of material in *Le Temps.*

52. Richmond *Dispatch,* April 6, 1864.

53. Lee Kennett, *Marching through Georgia: The Story of Soldiers and Civilians during Sherman's Campaign* (New York: HarperCollins, 1995), p. 12.

54. McPherson, *What They Fought For,* p. 18.

2. Nationalism

1. For an interpretation clearly influenced by the Vietnam War, see Robert L. Kerby, "Why the Confederacy Lost," *Review of Politics* 35 (July 1973), which argued that "the Confederacy's 'conservative revolution' suffered precisely because the nationalism of its old-line leaders did not coincide with either their own states' rights rhetoric or the states' rights beliefs and expectations of their people" (p. 332). See also Chapter 7 of Jeffrey Rogers Hummel, *Emancipating Slaves, Enslaving Free Men: A History of the American Civil War* (Chicago: Open Court Publishing, 1996), which drew heavily on Kerby's analysis. For an interesting rumination about similarities and differences between the United States efforts against the Confederacy and in Vietnam, see Stewart Alsop, "Will Westmoreland Elect Johnson?" in *Saturday Evening Post* 241 (January 13, 1968): 11.

2. On Washington and his army, see Don Higginbotham, *The War for American Independence: Military Attitudes, Policies, and Practice, 1763–1789* (New York: Macmillan, 1971), pp. 263–265; Don Higginbotham, *George Washington and the American Military Tradition* (Athens: University of Georgia Press, 1985), pp. 70–105; and Charles Royster, *A Revolutionary People at War: The Continental Army and American Character, 1775–1783* (Chapel Hill: University of North Carolina Press, 1979), pp. 255–262. John M. Murrin has offered a brilliant, and lamentably as yet unpublished, comparative discussion of American revolutionary and Confederate nationalism in "War, Revolution, and Nation-

Making: The American Revolution versus the American Civil War" (ms. dated September 1994, supplied to the author by Professor Murrin).

3. Limitations of space prevent a discussion of the large literature on nationalism, beyond pointing out that the work of Benedict Anderson, Eric Hobsbawm, Clifford Geertz, and others has been widely influential. The applicability of much of this scholarship to the Confederate example would make an excellent subject for another series of essays. In *The Creation of Confederate Nationalism: Ideology and Identity in the Civil War South* (Baton Rouge: Louisiana State University Press, 1988), p. 5, Drew Gilpin Faust raised a useful point concerning Geertz: "I would guess that most of the scholars who have cited Geertz's essay would not even remember that it includes a substantive treatment of Indonesian nationalism. Certainly in the case of scholarship on the American South, where Geertz's influence has been as deeply felt as in any other area of American history, few questions have arisen about the relevance of his work to the study of Confederate thought." For an excellent introduction to the topic of American nationalism, see Peter J. Parish, "An Exception to Most of the Rules: What Made American Nationalism Different in the Mid-Nineteenth Century?", *Prologue: Quarterly of the National Archives* 27 (Fall 1995): 219–229. Parish observed that many prominent scholars writing about nationalism, including Anderson and Hobsbawm, virtually ignored the mid-nineteenth-century United States; he similarly ignored the Confederacy. In "War, Revolution, and Nation-Making," p. 43, John Murrin concluded, "The effort to conquer the Confederacy placed fewer internal strains on northern society than on southern. For that reason Union nationalism could triumph over its Confederate rival even though, in objective terms, it was probably a weaker force during the years of actual warfare. With far more resources to draw upon, it never had to endure the Confederacy's astronomical losses. Had it faced such a crisis, it probably would have lost the war."

4. Frank E. Vandiver, *Their Tattered Flags: The Epic of the Confederacy* (New York: Harper's Magazine Press, 1970), pp. 156–157; Emory M. Thomas, "Reckoning with Rebels," in Harry P. Owens and James J. Cooke, eds., *The Old South in the Crucible of War* (Jackson: University Press of Mississippi, 1983), pp. 9–10, 12. Thomas's essay distills the principal arguments in his book *The Confederate Nation, 1861–1865* (New York: Harper & Row, 1979). See also Richard Franklin Bensel, *Yankee Leviathan: The Origins of Central State Authority in America, 1859–1877* (New York: Cambridge University Press, 1990),

which highlighted the impressive centralizing tendencies of the Confederacy and questioned the notion that white southerners on principle opposed expanding central authority. "It would appear that the South's opposition to the North's industrial and commercial policies provided the impetus for both the region's opposition to a strong American state in the Union and support for a centralized Confederate regime after secession," noted Bensel. "Southern support for a strong Confederate and a weak American state (before and after the Civil War until the end of Reconstruction) can thus be viewed as a consistent strategy intended to minimize the anticipated deleterious impact of the northern industrial program on the plantation South" (pp. 95–96). In *"A Government of Our Own": The Making of the Confederacy* (New York: Free Press, 1994), William C. Davis stressed that delegates to the provisional Confederate Congress in Montgomery, Alabama, in early 1861 considered themselves representatives of sovereign states—an argument that suggests war and increasing sacrifice promoted stronger national ties.

5. Faust, *Creation of Confederate Nationalism,* pp. 6–7, 22, 42, 60, 84.

6. Paul D. Escott, "The Failure of Confederate Nationalism: The Old South's Class System in the Crucible of War," in Owens and Cooke, *Old South in the Crucible of War,* pp. 16, 20.

7. Lawrence N. Powell and Michael S. Wayne, "Self-Interest and the Decline of Confederate Nationalism," in Owens and Cooke, *Old South in the Crucible of War,* pp. 32–33; Paul D. Escott, *After Secession: Jefferson Davis and the Failure of Confederate Nationalism* (Baton Rouge: Louisiana State University Press, 1978), p. 272.

8. Richard E. Beringer, Herman Hattaway, Archer Jones, and William N. Still, Jr., *Why the South Lost the Civil War* (Athens: University of Georgia Press, 1986), pp. 66, 425–426; Kenneth M. Stampp, "The Southern Road to Appomattox," in Kenneth M. Stampp, *The Imperiled Union: Essays on the Background of the Civil War* (New York: Oxford University Press, 1980), pp. 255–256, 259–260. Whether white southerners abandoned feelings of Confederate nationalism immediately after the war is a question that lies beyond the scope of this essay. It is sufficient to state that although the unambiguous military verdict of their four-year struggle convinced them they would have no new nation, for decades after Appomattox they sought through the Lost Cause movement to maintain an identity tied to their Confederate war and distinct in some ways from the American mainstream. On this topic, see Charles Reagan Wilson, *Baptized in Blood: The Religion of*

the Lost Cause, 1865–1920 (Athens: University of Georgia Press, 1980), and Gaines M. Foster, *Ghosts of the Confederacy: Defeat, the Lost Cause, and the Emergence of the New South, 1865 to 1913* (New York: Oxford University Press, 1987). In an observation directly pertinent to Stampp's arguments, Wilson wrote that the war ended white southern hopes for a separate political identity, "but the dream of a separate Southern identity did not die in 1865. A Southern political nation was not to be, and the people of Dixie came to accept that; but the dream of a cohesive Southern people with a separate cultural identity replaced the original longing. The cultural dream replaced the political dream: the South's kingdom was to be of culture, not of politics" (p. 1).

9. David M. Potter, "The Historian's Use of Nationalism and Vice Versa," in David M. Potter, *The South and the Sectional Conflict* (Baton Rouge: Louisiana State University Press, 1968), pp. 43, 45, 63. Potter's incisive essay remains the best exploration of the dangers inherent in exploring the topic of Confederate nationalism.

10. Beringer and others, *Why the South Lost,* p. 66; Stampp, "The Southern Road to Appomattox," p. 258; Reid Mitchell, "The Perseverance of the Soldiers," in Gabor S. Boritt, ed., *Why the Confederacy Lost* (New York: Oxford University Press, 1992), p. 124; Escott, *After Secession,* p. 272; Powell and Wayne, "Self Interest and the Decline of Confederate Nationalism," pp. 32–33. In *The Creation of Confederate Nationalism,* p. 3, Drew Gilpin Faust commented on this phenomenon: "Scholars have continued to fear that accepting the reality of Confederate nationalism would somehow imply legitimacy." It would be interesting to know whether these scholars would balk at the proposition that racism and white supremacy buttressed nationalism among white South Africans during the mid-twentieth century.

11. Although the sample was not a scientific one, it included soldiers and civilians from every Confederate state, officers and enlisted men, political figures, and slaveholders and nonslaveholders. The large majority of witnesses were slaveholders.

12. For good introductions to the subject of soldier loyalty to the Confederacy, see Chapter 1 of James M. McPherson, *What They Fought For, 1861–1865* (Baton Rouge: Louisiana State University Press, 1994), and Reid Mitchell, "The Creation of Confederate Loyalties," in Robert H. Abzug and Stephen E. Maizlish, eds., *New Perspectives on Race and Slavery in America: Essays in Honor of Kenneth M. Stampp* (Lexington: University Press of Kentucky, 1986).

13. For the view that military service promoted especially strong nationalistic feelings among soldiers, see Mitchell, "Creation of Confederate Loyalties," pp. 99–100, and Bell I. Wiley, *The Road to Appomattox* (Memphis: Memphis State College Press, 1956), pp. 74–75. For a dissenting view, see Michael Barton, "Did the Confederacy Change Southern Soldiers? Some Obvious and Some Unobtrusive Measures," in Owens and Cooke, *Old South in the Crucible of War*.

14. John F. Shaffner to Carrie Fries, December 26, 1862, in William Kelsey McDaid, "'Four Years of Arduous Service': The History of the Branch-Lane Brigade in the Civil War" (Ph.D. diss., Michigan State University, 1987), p. 161; John Andrew Ramsey to his cousin, December 17, 1862, John Andrew Ramsey Papers (no. 3534), SHC; Elisha Franklin Paxton to his wife, January 17, 1863, in Elisha Franklin Paxton, *The Civil War Letters of General Frank "Bull" Paxton: A Lieutenant of Lee and Jackson,* ed. John Gallatin Paxton (Hillsboro, Tex.: Hill Junior College Press, 1978), p. 71.

15. Marion Hill Fitzpatrick to Amanda Olive Elizabeth White Fitzpatrick, April 10, 1864, in Marion Hill Fitzpatrick, *Letters to Amanda, from Sergeant Major Marion Hill Fitzpatrick, Company K, 45th Georgia Regiment, Thomas' Brigade, Wilcox Division, Hill's Corps, CSA to His Wife Amanda Olive Elizabeth White Fitzpatrick, 1862–1865,* ed. Henry Mansel Hammock (Nashville, Tenn.: Champion Resources, 1982), p. 125; Thomas J. Goree to Sarah Williams Kittrell Goree, April 26, 1864, in Thomas J. Goree, *Longstreet's Aide: The Civil War Letters of Major Thomas J. Goree,* ed. Thomas W. Cutrer (Charlottesville: University Press of Virginia, 1995), pp. 122–123; Alexander G. MacArthur to Cousin Mary, March 5, 1864, C. W. MacArthur typescripts (Georgia no. 7), Kennesaw Mountain National Battlefield Park, Kennesaw, Georgia.

16. William Mason Smith to Mrs. William Mason Smith, April 1, 1864, Mrs. William Mason Smith to William Mason Smith, April 1864, in Daniel E. Huger Smith, Alice R. Huger Smith, and Arney R. Childs, eds., *Mason Smith Family Letters, 1860–1868* (Columbia: University of South Carolina Press, 1950), pp. 87–88.

17. Belle Edmondson, *A Lost Heroine of the Confederacy: The Diaries and Letters of Belle Edmondson,* ed. William Galbraith and Loretta Galbraith (Jackson: University Press of Mississippi, 1990), p. 81; Georgiana Gholson Walker, *The Private Journal of Georgiana Gholson Walker 1862–1865, with Selections from the Post-War Years, 1865–1876,* ed. Dwight Franklin Henderson (Tuscaloosa, Ala.: Confederate Publishing Co., 1963), pp. 73–74

(entry for March 7, 1864); Susan Emiline Jeffords Caldwell to Lycurgus Washington Caldwell, April 22, 1864, in J. Michael Welton, ed., *"My Heart is So Rebellious": The Caldwell Letters, 1861–1865* (Warrenton, Va.: Fauquier National Bank, n.d.), p. 218.

18. Irene Bell, Annie Samuels, and others to Secretary of War Seddon, December 2, 1864, quoted in Jane Ellen Schultz, "Women at the Front: Gender and Genre in Literature of the American Civil War" (Ph.D. diss., University of Michigan, 1988), p. 271; Emma LeConte, *When the World Ended: The Diary of Emma LeConte,* ed. Earl Schenck Miers (New York: Oxford University Press, 1957), p. 90.

19. W. C. Corsan, *Two Months in the Confederate States: An Englishman's Travels through the South,* ed. Benjamin H. Trask (1863; reprint, Baton Rouge: Louisiana State University Press, 1996), p. 91.

20. Ibid., p. 16; Ann E. Hope to "Dear Aunt," June 22, 1863, Peek Family Papers, SHC; Jane Howison Beale, *The Journal of Jane Howison Beale of Fredericksburg, Virginia, 1850–1862,* ed. Barbara P. Willis and Robert K. Krick (Fredericksburg: Historic Fredericksburg, 1979), p. 43 (entry for May 14, 1862).

21. A. J. Neal to his mother, July 23, 1864, in Mills Lane, ed., *"Dear Mother: Don't grieve about me. If I get killed, I'll only be dead": Letters from Georgia Soldiers in the Civil War* (Savannah, Ga.: Beehive Press, 1977), p. 321; R. E. Lee to Agnes Lee, December 26, 1862, in R. E. Lee, *The Wartime Papers of R. E. Lee,* ed. Clifford Dowdey and Louis H. Manarin (Boston: Little, Brown, 1961), p. 382; William A. Blair, "Barbarians at Fredericksburg's Gate: The Impact of the Union Army on Civilians," in Gary W. Gallagher, ed., *The Fredericksburg Campaign: Decision on the Rappahannock* (Chapel Hill: University of North Carolina Press, 1995), pp. 156–159; Corsan, *Two Months in the Confederate States,* p. 91.

22. Susan Bradford Eppes, *Through Some Eventful Years* (1926; reprint, Gainesville: University of Florida Press, 1968), p. 241 (diary entry for August 8, 1864); Richard H. Dulany to Mary Carter Dulany, July 5, 1864, in Margaret Ann Vogtsberger, ed., *The Dulanys of Welbourne: A Family in Mosby's Confederacy* (Berryville, Va.: Rockbridge Publishing Co., 1995), p. 169; Frances Addison Carter Dulany diary, June 15, 1864, in Vogtsberger, *Dulanys of Welbourne,* p. 164; Edward W. Cade to Allie Ann Smith Cade, November 19, 1863, in John Q. Anderson, *A Texas Surgeon in the C.S.A.* (Tuscaloosa, Ala.: Confederate Publishing Co., 1957), p. 81.

23. Raimundo Luraghi, *The Rise and Fall of the Plantation South* (New York: New Viewpoints, 1978), pp. 142–143; Robert F. Durden, *The Gray and the Black: The Confederate Debate on Emancipation* (Baton Rouge: Louisiana State University Press, 1972), pp. vii–viii. Durden observed that Lee's support for arming black men "apparently turned the tide of opinion, in and out of Congress" (p. 206). For resistance to emancipation in the North, see Forrest G. Wood, *Black Scare: The Racist Response to Emancipation and Reconstruction* (Berkeley: University of California Press, 1968). In *The Confederate Republic: A Revolution against Politics* (Chapel Hill: University of North Carolina Press, 1994), pp. 287–292, George C. Rable evaluated the debate over arming slaves in terms of "nationalists" who favored the proposal and "libertarians" who opposed it as another attempt by the central government to extend its power.

24. Clarence L. Mohr, *On the Threshold of Freedom: Masters and Slaves in Civil War Georgia* (Athens: University of Georgia Press, 1986), pp. 278–279; John B. Gordon to Walter H. Taylor, February 18, 1865, in *OR,* ser. 1, vol. 51, pt. 2, p. 1063. For a careful discussion of sentiment within the Army of Northern Virginia, see J. Tracy Power, "From the Wilderness to Appomattox: Life in Lee's Army of Northern Virginia, May 1864–April 1865," 2 vols. (Ph.D. diss., University of South Carolina, 1993), vol. 2, pp. 482–492. Power concluded that "while many, perhaps most, members of the army did indeed support the plan, they did so recognizing that the measure was one born out of necessity rather than choice" (p. 489).

25. Montgomery (Alabama) *Weekly Mail,* September 9, 1863, reprinting the Jackson *Mississippian* (date unspecified), quoted in Durden, *The Gray and the Black,* pp. 30–31.

26. Beringer and others, *Why the South Lost,* pp. 425–426; Catherine Ann Devereux Edmondston, *"Journal of a Secesh Lady": The Diary of Catherine Ann Devereux Edmondston, 1860–1866,* ed. Beth Gilbert Crabtree and James W. Patton (Raleigh: North Carolina Division of Archives and History, 1979), pp. 653, 696.

27. Escott, "Failure of Confederate Nationalism," pp. 18–19; Escott, *After Secession,* p. 197; Beringer and others, *Why the South Lost,* pp. 66, 64.

28. For a dissenting view about Lee's stature during the war, see Thomas L. Connelly, *The Marble Man: Robert E. Lee and His Image in American Society* (New York: Alfred A. Knopf, 1977).

29. Jefferson Davis to Robert E. Lee, August 11, 1863, in Jefferson Davis, *Jefferson Davis*

Constitutionalist: His Letters, Papers and Speeches, ed. Dunbar Rowland, 10 vols. (Jackson: Mississippi Department of Archives and History, 1923), vol. 5, pp. 588–590. For examples of interest in Lee's army among Confederates far from Virginia, see Edmondson, *Lost Heroine;* Kate Stone, *Brokenburn: The Journal of Kate Stone, 1861–1868,* ed. John Q. Anderson (Baton Rouge: Louisiana State University Press, 1955); and Felix Pierre Poché, *A Louisiana Confederate: Diary of Felix Pierre Poché,* ed. Edwin C. Bearss (Natchitoches: Louisiana Studies Institute of Northwestern State University of Louisiana, 1972).

30. Lynchburg *Virginian,* May 12, 1863; Arthur James Lyon Fremantle, *Three Months in the Southern States: April–June, 1863* (1863; reprint, Lincoln: University of Nebraska Press, 1991), p. 248; Edmondston, *Journal of a Secesh Lady,* p. 576; LeConte, *Diary,* p. 77; Mary Washington (Cabell) Early diary, April 4, 1865, Early Family Papers, VHS.

31. William Ransom Johnson Pegram to Mary Evans (Pegram) Anderson, July 21, 1864, Pegram-Johnson-McIntosh Papers, VHS; J. B. Jones, *A Rebel War Clerk's Diary at the Confederate Capital,* 2 vols. (1866; reprint, Alexandria, Va.: Time-Life Books, 1982), vol. 2, pp. 370–372 (entries for December 31, 1864, and January 1, 1865).

32. Jefferson Davis to James F. Johnson and Hugh W. Sheffey (president pro tempore of the Virginia Senate and speaker of the Virginia House of Delegates), January 18, 1865, in Davis, *Jefferson Davis,* vol. 6, p. 453; John Hampden Chamberlayne to Martha Burwell Chamberlayne, February 13, 1865, in C. G. Chamberlayne, ed., *Ham Chamberlayne—Virginian: Letters and Papers of an Artillery Officer in the War for Southern Independence, 1861–1865* (1932; reprint, Wilmington, N.C.: Broadfoot, 1992), p. 308; Edward O. Guerrant diary, February 23, 1865, SHC.

33. R. E. Lee to Mary Custis Lee, December 25, 1861, Lee to George Washington Custis Lee, December 29, 1861, Lee to Mary Custis Lee, December 25, 1862, June 19, 1864, in Lee, *Wartime Papers,* pp. 95–96, 98, 379–380, 793.

34. General Orders no. 7, January 22, 1864, in ibid., p. 659; Richmond *Enquirer,* February 5, 1864; Jones, *Diary,* vol. 2, p. 137.

35. R. E. Lee to Jefferson Davis, July 31, 1863, in Lee, *Wartime Papers,* pp. 564–565; Edgeworth Bird to Sallie Bird, July 19, August 28, 1863, in John Rozier, ed., *The Granite Farm Letters: The Civil War Correspondence of Edgeworth and Sallie Bird* (Athens: University of Georgia Press, 1988), pp. 125, 145; Reuben Allen Pierson to William H. Pierson, March 22, 1864, Pierson Papers, Tulane University, New Orleans; Ezekiel D. Graham to

Laura Mann, September 14, 1864, in possession (in 1987) of H. R. Shanton Granger, New York City.

36. Richard H. Dulany to Mary Dulany, June 8, 1864, in Vogtsberger, *Dulanys of Welbourne,* p. 160; James Keith to Juliet (Chilton) Keith, November 16, 1864, Keith Family Papers, VHS.

37. Clement A. Evans diary, January 18–28, 1864, in Clement Anselm Evans, *Intrepid Warrior: Clement Anselm Evans, Confederate General from Georgia, Life, Letters and Diaries of the War Years,* ed. Robert Grier Stephens, Jr. (Dayton, Ohio: Morningside, 1992), pp. 341–342; S. G. Pryor to Penelope Tyson Pryor, August 6, 1863, in Charles R. Adams, Jr., ed., *A Post of Honor: The Pryor Letters, 1861–63: Letters from Capt. S. G. Pryor, Twelfth Georgia Regiment and His Wife, Penelope Tyson Pryor* (Fort Valley, Ga.: Garret Publications, 1989), p. 385; Ted Barclay to "Dear Sister," February 22, 1864, in Ted Barclay, *Ted Barclay, Liberty Hall Volunteers: Letters from the Stonewall Brigade (1861–1864),* ed. Charles W. Turner (Natural Bridge, Va.: Rockbridge Publishing Co., 1992), p. 128.

38. Benjamin H. Freeman of the 44th North Carolina Infantry was typical of those who believed they would be kept in the ranks whether or not they reenlisted voluntarily: "Pa we have all Reinlisted for the 'War,'" he wrote on February 19, 1864. "We had to do it and I thought I would come on as a patriot soldier of the South[.] We are soldiers and we have to stay as long as there is any 'war[.]' [T]here is no way to escape it." Benjamin H. Freeman, *The Confederate Letters of Benjamin H. Freeman,* ed. Stuart T. Wright (Hicksville, N.Y.: Exposition Press, 1974), p. 34. Lt. Burwell T. Cotton of the 34th North Carolina Infantry expressed the same thought more succinctly in a letter to his sister on February 23, 1864: "Our Regt. reenlisted with the exception of a few recruits but no difference for that we are in for life or the war." Michael W. Taylor, ed., *The Cry Is War, War, War: The Civil War Correspondence of Lts. Burwell Thomas Cotton and George Job Huntley, 34th Regiment North Carolina State Troops* (Dayton, Ohio: Morningside, 1994), p. 166.

39. General Orders no. 19, Adjutant and Inspector General's Office, signed by Jefferson Davis, February 10, 1864, in *OR,* ser. 4, vol. 3, pp. 104–105; Richmond *Enquirer,* January 30, February 6, 1864.

40. Kate Cumming, *The Journal of a Confederate Nurse, 1862–1865,* ed. Richard B. Harwell (Savannah, Ga.: Beehive Press, 1975), p. 177 (entry for March 22, 1864); Walker, *Private Journal,* p. 69 (entry for February 18, 1864); Emma Holmes, *The Diary of Miss Emma*

Holmes, 1861–1866, ed. John F. Marszalek (Baton Rouge: Louisiana State University Press, 1979), p. 339 (entry for February 20, 1864).

41. Power, "From the Wilderness to Appomattox," vol. 2, pp. 475–477. In his discussion of these resolutions, Power observed that, as during the previous spring, some units exhibited more enthusiasm than others. Confederate deserters told Federals the meetings that spawned the resolutions were "presided over by the colonels of regiments"; the men feared speaking their true mind at these gatherings, "and the consequence is that it is taken for granted and declared by the officers that they are in favor of fighting it out" (vol. 2, p. 481).

42. Richmond *Dispatch,* February 17, 1865.

43. David Pierson to William H. Pierson, May 9, 1865, Pierson Family Papers, Tulane University, New Orleans; Sarah Strickler Fife Diary, Alderman Library, University of Virginia, Charlottesville; Eppes, *Through Some Eventful Years,* p. 270 (diary entry for April 10, 1865).

44. Peter S. Carmichael, "The Last Generation: Slaveholders' Sons and Southern Identity, 1850–1865" (Ph.D. diss., Pennsylvania State University, 1996), took a step in this direction. Carmichael's findings suggested a strong sense of southern and later Confederate identity among these young men. For extensive data concerning the field-grade officers in Lee's army, see Robert K. Krick, *Lee's Colonels: A Biographical Register of the Field Officers of the Army of Northern Virginia,* 4th ed., rev. (Dayton, Ohio: Morningside, 1992). For the median and average ages, see p. 19.

45. Among scholars who have noted the influence of army officers is Reid Mitchell, who wrote, "With the exception of Jefferson Davis, the Confederate authorities who inspired the most devotion both during the Civil War and after were the army officers." Mitchell, "Creation of Confederate Loyalties," p. 99.

46. The degree to which antebellum white southerners thought in terms of a separate slaveholding republic is a fascinating question beyond the scope of this book. Anyone interested in this topic should consult John McCardell, *The Idea of a Southern Nation: Southern Nationalists and Southern Nationalism, 1830–1860* (New York: W. W. Norton, 1979), pp. 336–337, wherein McCardell explored developing southern nationalist sentiment in the antebellum South. "Proceeding from a general commitment to the Constitution and a set of shared experiences in the Revolution," he concluded, "Americans moved

in different directions in attempting to work out their national purpose. Their disputes became subsumed by the slavery issue, out of which sprang sectional ideological configurations that eventually proved incompatible . . . By 1860 a large number of Southerners were convinced that their interests and those of the nation at large—which was controlled by a Northern and seemingly hostile majority—were incompatible. They decided that only in a separate Southern nation could they preserve their constitutional rights. Reluctantly they broke up the Union they had long cherished and served." Also useful is James M. McPherson's "Antebellum Southern Exceptionalism: A New Look at An Old Question," *Civil War History* 29 (September 1983): 230–244, which suggested that the antebellum southern vision of America departed less from the revolutionary model than did that of the North. "Thus when secessionists protested in 1861 that they were acting to preserve traditional rights and values," stated McPherson, "they were correct. They fought to protect their constitutional liberties against the perceived Northern threat to overthrow them. The South's concept of republicanism had not changed in three-quarters of a century; the North's had. With complete sincerity the South fought to preserve its version of the republic of the founding fathers—a government of limited powers that protected the rights of property and whose constituency comprised an independent gentry and yeomanry of the white race undisturbed by large cities, heartless factories, restless free workers, and class conflict" (p. 243).

47. Stephen Dodson Ramseur to David Schenck, November 8, 1856, Stephen Dodson Ramseur Papers, SHC; Charles C. Jones, Jr., to Rev. and Mrs. C. C. Jones (his parents), November 8, 1856, in Robert Manson Myers, ed., *The Children of Pride: A True Story of Georgia and the Civil War* (New Haven: Yale University Press, 1972), pp. 261–262.

48. Krick, *Lee's Colonels,* p. 20; *The Address of the Southern Rights Association, of the University of Virginia to the Young Men of the South* (Charlottesville: John Alexander, Printer, 1851), pp. 6–7. This address appeared several years before the arrival at the University of Virginia of professors Albert Taylor Bledsoe and George Frederick Holmes, two strong proslavery thinkers who doubtless influenced students in the late 1850s. On Bledsoe and Holmes, see Eugene D. Genovese, *The Slaveholders' Dilemma: Freedom and Progress in Southern Conservative Thought, 1820–1860* (Columbia: University of South Carolina Press, 1992), and Drew Gilpin Faust, *A Sacred Circle: The Dilemma of the Intellectual in the Old South, 1840–1860* (Baltimore: Johns Hopkins University Press, 1977). *Southern Planter* 16

(May 1856): 148–153, and 16 (July 1856): 193–197, contains an admiring analysis of Bledsoe's proslavery arguments and a long response by Bledsoe.

49. John L. Buchanan, "The Conflicts of Parties," *Southern Repertory and College Review* 4 (December 1855): 144; Walter Monteiro, *Address Delivered before the Neotrophian Society of the Hampton Academy, on the Twenty-Eighth of July, 1857* (Richmond: H. K. Ellyson, Printer, 1857), pp. 15–18.

50. "Bian," "Southern Education for Southern Youth," *Hampden Sidney Magazine* 1 (March 1859): 84–85; G. W. W. M. Simms, "The South," *Southern Repertory and College Review* 3 (June 1854): 222, 226.

51. Edward Porter Alexander to Mary Clifford (Alexander) Hull, November 11, 1860, in Marion Boggs Alexander, ed., *The Alexander Letters, 1787–1900* (1910; reprint, Athens: University of Georgia Press, 1980), p. 220; Thomas Jewett Goree to Sarah Williams Kittrell Goree (his mother), December 13, 1860, January 22, 1861, in Goree, *Longstreet's Aide,* pp. 4–5.

52. Gary W. Gallagher, *Stephen Dodson Ramseur: Lee's Gallant General* (Chapel Hill: University of North Carolina Press, 1985), p. 29; William Dorsey Pender to Fanny Pender, March 14, April 3, May 4, 1861, in William Dorsey Pender, *The General to His Lady: The Civil War Letters of William Dorsey Pender to Fanny Pender,* ed. William W. Hassler (Chapel Hill: University of North Carolina Press, 1965), pp. 9, 14, 18.

53. Henry King Burgwyn, Jr., to his father, January 11, 1861, and to his mother, December 9, 15, 1860, quoted in Archie K. Davis, *Boy Colonel of the Confederacy: The Life and Times of Henry King Burgwyn, Jr.* (Chapel Hill: University of North Carolina Press, 1985), pp. 59, 49–50.

54. Jennings C. Wise, *The Military History of the Virginia Military Institute from 1839 to 1865* (Lynchburg, Va.: J. P. Bell, 1915), pp. 126–128; Ollinger Crenshaw, *General Lee's College: The Rise and Growth of Washington and Lee University* (New York: Random House, 1969), p. 120; Henry Lenoir to his mother, January 20, 186[1], Lenoir Family Papers, VHS; Philip Alexander Bruce, *History of the University of Virginia, 1819–1919,* 4 vols. (New York: Macmillan, 1921), vol. 3, p. 264. For a discussion of the substantial contribution VMI alumni made to Lee's army, see Richard M. McMurry, *Two Great Rebel Armies: An Essay in Confederate Military History* (Chapel Hill: University of North Carolina Press, 1989), pp. 100–102. McMurry notes that 819 VMI men served as Confederate military

officers (including 18 generals and 95 colonels), virtually all of them in the Army of Northern Virginia.

55. John Hampden Chamberlayne to George W. Bagby, February 1, 1861, in Chamberlayne, ed., *Ham Chamberlayne—Virginian,* p. xxxiii; Peter S. Carmichael, *Lee's Young Artillerist: William R. J. Pegram* (Charlottesville: University Press of Virginia, 1995), pp. 25–26.

56. Alexander Swift Pendleton to William Nelson Pendleton, February 25, 1862, quoted in W. G. Bean, "The Valley Campaign of 1862 as Revealed in the Letters of Sandie Pendleton," *Virginia Magazine of History and Biography* 78 (July 1970): 332.

57. William McWillie Notebooks, Mississippi Department of Archives and History, Jackson. A member of General Richard H. Anderson's staff in 1864, McWillie recorded notes of conversations in which he participated and statements made to him by other officers.

58. Stephen Dodson Ramseur to Ellen Richmond Ramseur, October 2, 1864, Ramseur Papers, SHC; James Keith to Sarah Agnes (Blackwell) Keith, October 18, 1864, Keith Family Papers, VHS.

59. Walter H. Taylor to Bettie Saunders, February 6, 1865, in Walter H. Taylor, *Lee's Adjutant: The Wartime Letters of Colonel Walter Herron Taylor, 1862–1865,* ed. R. Lockwood Tower (Columbia: University of South Carolina Press, 1995), p. 221; William Ransom Johnson Pegram to Mary Evans (Pegram) Anderson, March 14, 1865, in James I. Robertson, Jr., ed., "'The Boy Artillerist': Letters of Colonel William Pegram, C.S.A.," *Virginia Magazine of History and Biography* 98 (April 1990): 257–258.

60. William Gordon McCabe to Mary Early, April 7, 1865, Early Family Papers, 1764–1956, VHS.

61. Walter Taylor to Bettie Saunders, February 16, 1865, in Taylor, *Lee's Adjutant,* pp. 223–224; John Hampden Chamberlayne to Lucy Parke (Chamberlayne) Bagby, March 29, 1865, in Chamberlayne, ed., *Ham Chamberlayne,* p. 316.

62. Pender, *General to His Lady,* pp. 259–261; Davis, *Boy Colonel,* pp. 331–337; Carmichael, *Lee's Young Artillerist,* pp. 163–167; William G. Bean, *Stonewall's Man: Sandie Pendleton* (Chapel Hill: University of North Carolina Press, 1959), pp. 210–211; Gallagher, *Ramseur,* pp. 161–162, 165.

63. William M. Norman, *A Portion of My Life: Being a Short & Imperfect History Written while a Prisoner of War on Johnson's Island 1864* (Winston-Salem, N.C.: J. F. Blair, 1959),

p. 183; William H. May, ms. recollection of the Civil War, p. 6, William H. May Papers, Alabama Department of Archives and History, Montgomery.

64. Lee frequently paid high tribute to his young officers. For a convenient collection of his comments, see Douglas Southall Freeman, *Lee's Lieutenants: A Study in Command,* 3 vols. (New York: Charles Scribner's Sons, 1942–1944).

65. For the argument that soldiers experienced alienation from the civilian population, see Mitchell, "Creation of Confederate Loyalties," pp. 98–99.

3. Military Strategy

1. On the roles of Davis and Lee in determining Confederate strategy, see Steven E. Woodworth's *Jefferson Davis and His Generals: The Failure of Confederate Command in the West* (Lawrence: University Press of Kansas, 1990) and *Davis and Lee at War* (Lawrence: University Press of Kansas, 1995), and William C. Davis's "Lee and Jefferson Davis," in Gary W. Gallagher, ed., *Lee the Soldier* (Lincoln: University of Nebraska Press, 1996), pp. 291–305. The best general discussion of Confederate strategy is in Herman Hattaway and Archer Jones, *How the North Won: A Military History of the Civil War* (Urbana: University of Illinois Press, 1983). Also useful are Thomas Lawrence Connelly and Archer Jones, *The Politics of Command: Factions and Ideas in Confederate Strategy* (Baton Rouge: Louisiana State University Press, 1973); Archer Jones, "Military Means, Political Ends: Strategy," in Gabor S. Boritt, ed., *Why the Confederacy Lost* (New York: Oxford University Press, 1992); and Chapter 4 of Alan T. Nolan, *Lee Considered: General Robert E. Lee and Civil War History* (Chapel Hill: University of North Carolina Press, 1991). These works present various opinions about the effectiveness of Confederate strategy.

2. On this point, see Jones, "Military Means, Political Ends: Strategy," pp. 75–76, and Frank E. Vandiver, "The Shifting Roles of Jefferson Davis," in Gary W. Gallagher, ed., *Essays on Southern History: Written in Honor of Barnes F. Lathrop* (Austin: The General Libraries of the University of Texas, 1980), p. 125. "In the end he lost and his cause went down to the fullest defeat," wrote Vandiver of Davis. But that does not mean the Confederate president favored a poor strategic plan: "His strategy lacked great originality or elegance, but it showed again how far he had come from prewar romanticism. His strategy was the offensive-defensive—a program fitted perfectly to southern conditions and

shortages and advantages. The weaker side must husband resources but never permanently yield initiative."

3. James M. McPherson identified four "major turning points, points of contingency when events moved in one direction but could well have moved in another": George B. McClellan's failure to capture Richmond in the spring and early summer of 1862, the Confederate strategic counteroffensive in the late summer and fall of that year, the summer of 1863 when Lee marched north into Pennsylvania, and Sherman's capture of Atlanta in September 1864. Each of these turning points brought a marked shift in morale behind the lines in the Union and the Confederacy, illustrating McPherson's point that "the will of either the northern or southern people was primarily a result of military victory rather than a cause of it." James M. McPherson, "American Victory, American Defeat," in Boritt, *Why the Confederacy Lost,* pp. 40–42.

4. See especially Hattaway and Jones, *How the North Won,* for analysis of the wartime debates among Confederates.

5. G. T. Beauregard, "The First Battle of Bull Run," in *B&L,* vol. 1, pp. 222–223; P. G. T. Beauregard to Thomas Jordan, n.d., 1868, quoted in T. Harry Williams, *P. G. T. Beauregard: Napoleon in Gray* (Baton Rouge: Louisiana State University Press, 1955), p. 305; Joseph E. Johnston, *Narrative of Military Operations Directed, during the Late War between the States* (1874; reprint, Bloomington: Indiana University Press, 1959), pp. 355–359, 363.

6. James Longstreet, "Lee's Invasion of Pennsylvania," in *B&L,* vol. 3, pp. 245–246. Longstreet's criticisms of Lee provoked a massive response from admirers of Lee. For the best discussion of this phenomenon, see William Garrett Piston, *Lee's Tarnished Lieutenant: James Longstreet and His Place in Southern History* (Athens: University of Georgia Press, 1987).

7. Grady McWhiney and Perry D. Jamieson, *Attack and Die: Civil War Military Tactics and the Southern Heritage* (University: University of Alabama Press, 1982), pp. xv, 6, 18. For an appreciation of the value of Lee's offensive instincts, see Chapter 2 of Joseph T. Glatthaar, *Partners in Command: The Relationships between Leaders in the Civil War* (New York: Free Press, 1994).

8. For a representative collection of opinions from the historical debate about Lee's generalship, see Gallagher, *Lee the Soldier.*

9. McWhiney and Jamieson, *Attack and Die,* pp. 70, 164–165; Thomas L. Connelly, "Robert E. Lee and the Western Confederacy: A Criticism of Lee's Strategic Ability," *Civil War History* 15 (June 1969): 130–131; Emory M. Thomas, *Robert E. Lee: A Biography* (New York: W. W. Norton, 1995), pp. 140–141, 226.

10. Nolan, *Lee Considered,* pp. 71, 101. See also George A. Bruce, "Lee and the Strategy of the Civil War," in Gallagher, *Lee the Soldier,* and J. F. C. Fuller, *Grant and Lee: A Study in Personality and Generalship* (1933; reprint, Bloomington: Indiana University Press, 1957).

11. Robert L. Kerby, "Why the Confederacy Lost," *The Review of Politics* 35 (July 1973): 331–332, 335, 339.

12. Jeffrey Rogers Hummel, *Emancipating Slaves, Enslaving Free Men: A History of the American Civil War* (Chicago: Open Court Publishing, 1996), pp. 179–180.

13. Richard E. Beringer, Herman Hattaway, Arches Jones, and William N. Still, Jr., *Why the South Lost the Civil War* (Athens: University of Georgia Press, 1986), pp. 436–438; Reid Mitchell, "The Perseverance of the Soldiers," in Boritt, *Why the Confederacy Lost,* pp. 124–125.

14. John M. Gates, "Indians and Insurrectos: The US Army's Experience with Insurgency," *Parameters: Journal of the US Army War College* 13 (March 1983): 60–61.

15. J. B. Jones, *A Rebel War Clerk's Diary at the Confederate States Capital,* 2 vols. (1866; reprint, Alexandria, Va.: Time-Life Books, 1982), vol. 1, p. 51.

16. Richmond *Dispatch,* January 3, 1862; Jones, *Diary,* vol. 1, p. 135; Macon *Journal & Messenger,* September 10, 1862.

17. Edward A. Pollard, *Southern History of the War: The First Year of the War* (1862; reprint, New York: Charles B. Richardson, 1864), p. 265; Jones, *Diary,* vol. 1, p. 124; [Judith W. McGuire], *Diary of a Southern Refugee during the War* (1867; reprint, Lincoln: University of Nebraska Press, 1995), pp. 102, 113. Pollard's four-volume *Southern History of the War* has a well deserved reputation for antipathy toward Jefferson Davis.

18. Mary Chesnut, *The Private Mary Chesnut: The Unpublished Civil War Diaries,* ed. C. Vann Woodward and Elisabeth Muhlenfeld (New York: Oxford University Press, 1984), pp. 129, 143, 162 (entries for August 19, 27, September 20, 1861); Catherine Ann Devereux Edmondston, *"Journal of a Secesh Lady": The Diary of Catherine Ann Devereux Edmondston, 1860–1866,* ed. Beth Gilbert Crabtree and James W. Patton (Raleigh: North Carolina Division of Archives and History, 1979), pp. 169, 189 (entries for May 6, June 8, 1862).

19. Pollard, *First Year of the War,* p. 168; Armistead L. Long, *Memoirs of Robert E. Lee: His Military and Personal History Embracing a Large Amount of Information Hitherto Unpublished* (1886; reprint, Secaucus, N. J.: Blue and Grey Press, 1983), p. 130; Edward Porter Alexander, *Fighting for the Confederacy: The Personal Recollections of General Edward Porter Alexander,* ed. Gary W. Gallagher (Chapel Hill: University of North Carolina Press, 1989), p. 90.

20. Richmond *Dispatch,* July 9, 1862; Edward A. Pollard, *Lee and His Lieutenants; Comprising the Early Life, Public Services, and Campaigns of General Robert E. Lee and His Companions in Arms, with a Record of their Campaigns and Heroic Deeds* (New York: E. B. Treat, 1867), p. 65.

21. William P. Snow, *Lee and His Generals* (1865; reprint, New York: Fairfax Press, 1982), p. 300; Charles C. Jones, Jr., to Rev. C. C. Jones, May 12, 1862, in Robert Manson Myers, ed., *The Children of Pride: A True Story of Georgia and the Civil War* (New Haven, Conn.: Yale University Press, 1972), p. 893; Jack King to his wife, July 19, 1864, in Mills Lane, ed., *"Dear Mother: Don't grieve about me. If I get killed, I'll only be dead": Letters from Georgia Soldiers in the Civil War* (Savannah, Ga.: Beehive Press, 1977), p. 258; Emma LeConte, *When the World Ended: The Diary of Emma LeConte,* ed. Early Schenck Miers (New York: Oxford University Press, 1957), p. 83 (entry for March 18, 1865).

22. Jubal A. Early, *The Campaigns of Gen. Robert E. Lee: An Address by Lieut. General Jubal A. Early, before Washington and Lee University, January 19th, 1872* (Baltimore: John Murphy, 1872), p. 37. Confederates frequently had bad luck with sieges even when they were the investing force. James Longstreet failed at Suffolk in the spring of 1863 and at Knoxville later that year, and Braxton Bragg's siege of Chattanooga ended in utter defeat in November 1863.

23. Thomas L. Livermore, *Numbers and Losses in the Civil War in America: 1861–1865* (1900; reprint, Bloomington: Indiana University Press, 1957), pp. 80–81; Edwin C. Bearss, *The Campaign for Vicksburg,* 3 vols. (Dayton, Ohio: Morningside, 1985–86), vol. 2, pp. 402–407, 515–517, 555–558, 642–651, 686–689. In a careful reckoning of losses during this phase of the Vicksburg campaign, Bearss gave the totals as 4,321 Federal and 5,891 Confederate casualties, noting that he lacked reports for many Confederate units. Figures from those commands would push Confederate casualties above 6,000.

24. Livermore, *Numbers and Losses,* pp. 119–120. The battle of Kennesaw Mountain,

where Sherman attacked Johnston's well-prepared defenses on June 27, 1864, added 2,051 Federal and 442 Confederate casualties to the totals.

25. McWhiney and Jamieson, *Attack and Die,* pp. 164–165.

26. Alan T. Nolan, "Confederate Leadership at Fredericksburg," in Gary W. Gallagher, ed., *The Fredericksburg Campaign: Decision on the Rappahannock* (Chapel Hill: University of North Carolina Press, 1995), p. 44; McWhiney and Jamieson, *Attack and Die,* p. 71.

27. For the argument that even Gettysburg did not tarnish appreciably Lee's reputation in the Confederacy, see Gary W. Gallagher, "Another Look at the Generalship of R. E. Lee," in Gary W. Gallagher, *Lee the Soldier,* and "Lee's Army Has Not Lost Any of Its Prestige: The Impact of Gettysburg on the Army of Northern Virginia and the Confederate Home Front," in Gary W. Gallagher, ed., *The Third Day at Gettysburg and Beyond* (Chapel Hill: University of North Carolina Press, 1994).

28. Nolan, *Lee Considered,* p. 81; Connelly, "Lee and the Western Confederacy," p. 118. The number of Confederates surrendered at Forts Henry and Donelson probably fell between 16,500 and 17,500, exceeding by 4,000–5,000 men the number of casualties at Chancellorsville. On the surrenders, see Ulysses S. Grant, *The Papers of Ulysses S. Grant,* ed. John Y. Simon, 21 vols. to date (Carbondale: Southern Illinois University Press, 1967–), vol. 4, p. 226, n.1, and Benjamin Franklin Cooling, *Forts Henry and Donelson: The Key to the Confederate Heartland* (Knoxville: University of Tennessee Press, 1987), p. 216.

29. Livermore's *Numbers and Losses,* pp. 86, 88–93, 96–99, which inflates Confederate casualties at Antietam by about 2,500, gives the following totals: Seven Days, 20,614 (3,478 killed in action); Second Manassas/Chantilly, 9,197 (1,481); South Mountain/Antietam, 16,409 (3,025); Fredericksburg, 5,309 (595); and Chancellorsville, 12,764 (1,665)—a total of 64,293 (10,244).

30. Lincoln (quoted by Noah Brooks) in James M. McPherson, *Battle Cry of Freedom: The Civil War Era* (New York: Oxford University Press, 1988), p. 645; Gideon Welles, *Diary of Gideon Welles: Secretary of the Navy under Lincoln and Johnson,* ed. Howard K. Beale, 3 vols. (New York: W. W. Norton, 1960), vol. 1. p. 293 (diary entry for May 6, 1863); Allan Nevins, *The War for the Union: War Becomes Revolution, 1862–1863* (New York: Charles Scribner's Sons, 1960), p. 450.

31. Charles P. Roland, *An American Iliad: The Story of the Civil War* (Lexington: University Press of Kentucky, 1991), p. 128. For representative comments about Lee's

being unbeatable, see Kate Stone, *Brokenburn: The Journal of Kate Stone, 1861–1868,* ed. John Q. Anderson (Baton Rouge: Louisiana State University Press, 1955), pp. 230, 248; and Felix Pierre Poché, *A Louisiana Confederate: The Diary of Felix Pierre Poché,* ed. Edwin C. Bearss (Natchitoches: Louisiana Studies Institute of Northwestern State University of Louisiana, 1972), p. 126.

32. McPherson, *Battle Cry of Freedom,* p. 645; James M. McPherson, *Ordeal by Fire: The Civil War and Reconstruction,* 2nd ed. (New York: McGraw-Hill, 1992), p. 322.

33. Thomas Conolly, *An Irishman in Dixie: Thomas Conolly's Diary of the Fall of the Confederacy,* ed. Nelson D. Lankford (Columbia: University of South Carolina Press, 1988), p. 52. Confederate newspapers contained remarkably little criticism of Lee's high casualties—in marked contrast to grumbling in the northern press about Grant's losses during campaigning in 1864.

34. Jefferson Davis, *Jefferson Davis Constitutionalist: His Letters, Papers and Speeches,* ed. Dunbar Rowland, 10 vols. (Jackson: Mississippi Department of Archives and History, 1923), vol. 6, p. 530; Kerby, "Why the Confederacy Lost," pp. 344–345.

35. Davis, *Jefferson Davis Constitutionalist,* vol. 6, p. 530.

36. Alexander, *Fighting for the Confederacy,* p. 532; R. E. Lee to Jefferson Davis, April 20, 1865, in R. E. Lee, *The Wartime Papers of R. E. Lee,* ed. Clifford Dowdey and Louis H. Manarin (Boston: Little, Brown, 1961), p. 939.

37. Jennings C. Wise, *The Military History of the Virginia Military Institute from 1839 to 1865* (Lynchburg, Va.: J. P. Bell, 1915), p. 24. Wise emphasized the influence of West Point on the early leaders at V.M.I., including Major Francis H. Smith, the Institute's initial superintendent: "The first official act of Major Smith was to confer with Colonel Thayer, the distinguished and successful Superintendent of West Point, for the purpose of securing suggestions from him, as well as samples of the uniforms, arms and equipment in use at the Academy" (p. 40). On the subject of military schools in the South, see also Chapter 8, "West Points of the South," in John Hope Franklin, *The Militant South, 1800–1861* (Cambridge: Harvard University Press, 1956); Gary R. Baker, *Cadets in Gray: The Story of the Cadets of the South Carolina Military Academy and the Cadet Rangers in the Civil War* (Columbia, S.C.: Palmetto Bookworks, 1989), pp. 1–10; and Richard M. McMurry, *Two Great Rebel Armies: An Essay in Confederate Military History* (Chapel Hill: University of North Carolina Press, 1989), pp. 98–105.

38. On the early war careers and strategic thinking of three officers prominent during the opening acts of the Confederate war, see T. Harry Williams, *P. G. T. Beauregard: Napoleon in Gray* (Baton Rouge: Louisiana State University Press, 1955), pp. 47–95; Charles P. Roland, *Albert Sidney Johnston: Soldier of Three Republics* (Austin: University of Texas Press, 1964), pp. 259–278; and Craig L. Symonds, *Joseph E. Johnston: A Civil War Biography* (New York: W. W. Norton, 1992), pp. 101–124.

39. Davis, *Jefferson Davis Constitutionalist,* vol. 5, pp. 51–52.

40. On this point, see Emory M. Thomas, *The Confederate Nation, 1861–1865* (New York: Harper & Row, 1979), p. 104.

41. Howard Jones, *Union in Peril: The Crisis over British Intervention in the Civil War* (Chapel Hill: University of North Carolina Press, 1992), pp. 182, 162–163, 1–2.

42. P. G. T. Beauregard to Col. A. Herman, September 4, 1861, quoted in Stan V. Henkels Auction House, *Catalogue 1148: The Beauregard Papers* (Philadelphia: Henkels, 1915), item 51; Thomas, *Confederate Nation,* pp. 221–222; Mary Jones to Charles C. Jones, Jr., December 19, 1862, in Myers, *Children of Pride,* p. 1001; Eliza Frances Andrews, *The War-Time Journal of a Georgia Girl, 1864–1865,* ed. Spencer Birdwell King (1908; reprint, Atlanta: Cherokee Publishing Co., 1976), p. 371 (diary entry for August 18, 1865).

43. Russell F. Weigley, *The American Way of War: A History of American Strategy and Military Policy* (New York: Macmillan, 1973), pp. 96–97; Allan R. Millett and Peter Maslowski, *For the Common Defense: A Military History of the United States of America* (New York: Free Press, 1984), p. 164.

44. Michael Fellman, *Inside War: The Guerrilla Conflict in Missouri during the American Civil War* (New York: Oxford University Press, 1989), p. xviii.

45. Donald E. Reynolds, *Editors Make War: Southern Newspapers in the Secession Crisis* (Nashville, Tenn.: Vanderbilt University Press, 1970), pp. 97–101; Clarence L. Mohr, *On the Threshold of Freedom: Masters and Slaves in Civil War Georgia* (Athens: University of Georgia Press, 1986), pp. 20–21, 49–51.

46. Betty Herndon Maury, *The Civil War Diary of Betty Herndon Maury (June 3, 1861–February 18, 1863),* ed. Robert A. Hodge (Fredericksburg, Va.: privately printed, 1985), p. 52 (entry for April 25, 1862); Steven V. Ash, *When the Yankees Came: Conflict and Chaos in the Occupied South, 1861–1865* (Chapel Hill: University of North Carolina Press, 1995), pp. 22–23.

47. Ash, *When the Yankees Came*, pp. 20–22.

48. John Ellis, *From the Barrel of a Gun: A History of Guerrilla, Revolutionary and Counter-Insurgency Warfare from the Romans to the Present* (Mechanicsburg, Pa.: Stackpole Books, 1995), p. 235.

49. Jefferson Davis to Joseph Davis, May 7, 1863, typescript provided by Jefferson Davis Association, Rice University, Houston, Texas; Jefferson Davis to Francis W. Pickens, August 1, 1862, summary in Jefferson Davis, *The Papers of Jefferson Davis,* ed. Lynda Lasswell Crist and others, 8 vols. to date (Baton Rouge: Louisiana State University Press, 1971–), vol. 8, p. 318.

50. For an excellent comparative evaluation of Lee and Confederate officers in the Western Theater, see McMurry, *Two Great Rebel Armies.*

4. Defeat

1. The Ku Klux Klan, rifle clubs, and other white groups that formed in the South during Reconstruction used violent means to achieve racial and political goals, but their actions did not represent a continuation of the Confederate war. These organizations did not seek to dismember the United States, and they mustered a relatively insignificant percentage of the South's white males and operated with minimal interstate cooperation. Employing the methods of thugs and assassins, they intimidated black and white Republicans and hastened the return of Democratic rule in some southern states. The most detailed discussion of violence during the postwar years is George C. Rable's *But There Was No Peace: The Role of Violence in the Politics of Reconstruction* (Athens: University of Georgia Press, 1984), which concludes that "by the time the federal government retreated from its reconstruction of the South, former Confederates had achieved through political terrorism what they had been unable to win with their armies—the freedom to order their own society and particularly race relations as they saw fit" (p. 1). But most white southerners in the late 1860s and 1870s almost certainly still considered slavery the ideal social and economic system within which to order race relations, and they had sought through secession and war to found a national government overtly dedicated to promoting a slave-based society. Four years of fighting had taught them the futility of a massive military effort to achieve such a republic. They settled for the more modest set

of goals described by Rable, using carefully applied incidents of violence to help realize them.

2. R. E. Lee, Special Order No. 9, April 10, 1865, in R. E. Lee, *The Wartime Papers of R. E. Lee,* ed. Clifford Dowdey and Louis H. Manarin (Boston: Little, Brown, 1961), p. 934; Catherine Ann Devereux Edmondston, *"Journal of a Secesh Lady": The Diary of Catherine Ann Devereux Edmondston, 1860–1866,* ed. Beth Gilbert Crabtree and James W. Patton (Raleigh: North Carolina Division of Archives and History, 1979), p. 713 (entry for June 26, 1865).

3. Sarah Hine to Charlotte Branch, February 10, 1866, in Mauriel Phillips Joslyn, ed., *Charlotte's Boys: Civil War Letters of the Branch Family of Savannah* (Berryville, Va.: Rockbridge Publishing Co., 1996), p. 310.

4. John T. Trowbridge, *The Desolate South, 1865–1866: A Picture of the Battlefields and of the Devastated Confederacy,* ed. Gordon Carroll (1866; reprint, New York: Duell, Sloan and Pearce, 1956), p. 74. Many Union dead suffered a similar fate—though most of them were gathered for burial in national cemeteries near the war's bloodiest battlegrounds. Southern women took the lead after the war in removing Confederate bodies from battlefields to cemeteries such as Hollywood in Richmond and Blandford in Petersburg, Virginia. On the removal of nearly 3,000 Confederate bodies from Gettysburg to Hollywood Cemetery in 1872–73, see Mary H. Mitchell, *Hollywood Cemetery: The History of a Southern Shrine* (Richmond: Virginia State Library, 1985), pp. 83–92.

5. J. B. Jones, *A Rebel War Clerk's Diary at the Confederate States Capital,* 2 vols. (1866; reprint, Alexandria, Va.: Time-Life Books, 1982), vol. 2, p. 470. Photographs of ruined southern cities have been published in many books. For Barnard's views, see Keith F. Davis, *George N. Barnard: Photographer of Sherman's Campaign* (Kansas City, Mo.: Hallmark Cards, 1990), especially plates 38, 44, 52, 53, 54, 55, 59, and 61. An excellent series on the ruins in Richmond is in Francis Trevelyan Miller, ed., *The Photographic History of the Civil War,* 10 vols. (New York: Review of Reviews, 1911), vol. 9, pp. 231, 306–307.

6. Arthur James Lyon Fremantle, *Three Months in the Southern States: April–June 1863* (1863; reprint, Lincoln: University of Nebraska Press, 1991), p. 223 (diary entry for June 21, 1863); Mobile *Register,* November 26, 1864.

7. Stephen V. Ash, *Middle Tennessee Society Transformed, 1860–1870: War and Peace in the Upper South* (Baton Rouge: Louisiana State University Press, 1988), pp. 85–86. Ash

made the point that "the principal agent of destruction in Middle Tennessee was not armed conflict per se but the Union army. Though the region was among the Civil War's most fought-over battlegrounds (Confederate armies contested it [in] 1862–63 and late 1864; smaller military forces and guerrillas did so throughout the war), relatively little damage resulted from actual combat between blue and gray regiments on the battlefield. Instead, the region's role as breadbasket of the Federal army and strategic gateway to the Deep South brought down upon it the full wrath of war" (p. 86).

8. George W. Guess to Mrs. Sarah Horton Cockrell, June 30, 1864, in "Civil War Letters, Colonel George W. Guess to Mrs. Sarah Horton Cockrell," bound volume of photostat copies with typescript title page (private edition of 12 copies made for the owner, Monroe F. Cockrell, Chicago, Ill., spring 1946), Center for American History, University of Texas, Austin.

9. Robert Garlick Hill Kean, *Inside the Confederate Government: The Diary of Robert Garlick Hill Kean,* ed. Edward Younger (New York: Oxford University Press, 1957), pp. 208, 210 (entry for June 1, 1865).

10. James A. Scott, *"Diary of a Private Soldier"* (n.p.: privately printed, n.d.), pp. 32–33 (entry probably made in late April 1865).

11. Elizabeth Pendleton Hardin, *The Private War of Lizzie Hardin: A Kentucky Confederate Girl's Diary of the Civil War in Kentucky, Virginia, Tennessee, Alabama, and Georgia,* ed. G. Glenn Clift (Frankfort: Kentucky Historical Society, 1963), pp. 241, 254 (entries for May 3, June 3, 1865).

12. Trowbridge, *The Desolate South,* pp. 91–92.

13. John Richard Dennett, *The South As It Is, 1865–1866,* ed. Henry M. Christman (Baton Rouge: Louisiana State University Press, 1965), p. 19; testimony of John C. Underwood before the Joint Committee on Reconstruction, January 31, 1866, U.S. Congress, *Report of the Joint Committee on Reconstruction, at the First Session Thirty-Ninth Congress* (Washington, D.C.: GPO, 1866), pp. 6–7.

14. Hardin, *Private War,* pp. 279–280 (entry for July 7, 1865).

15. Anne S. Frobel, *The Civil War Diary of Anne S. Frobel of Wilton Hill in Virginia,* ed. Mary H. and Dallas M. Lancaster (Florence, Ala.: n.p., 1986), pp. 182–183 (entries for July 1, 2, 4, 1865).

16. Mathew Woodruff, *A Union Soldier in the Land of the Vanquished: The Diary of*

Sergeant Mathew Woodruff, June–December 1865, ed. F. N. Boney (University: University of Alabama Press, 1969), pp. 48–49 (entry for October 17, 1865).

17. Despite an imposing body of evidence to the contrary, the idea of relatively easy reconciliation after the Civil War has enjoyed wide appeal. Americans have embraced the image of northerners and southerners forgiving one another and paying tribute to each other's wartime bravery and self-sacrifice (an image closely related to that of essentially *American* soldiers from North and South fraternizing during the war). The final episode of Ken Burns's influential documentary on the Civil War encouraged such a view by highlighting photographs and grainy motion picture footage of aging veterans clasping hands at Gettysburg, revisiting other battle sites where both sides had demonstrated courage and devotion to their respective causes, and honoring one another at funerals. The notion that former Confederates moved rapidly toward reconciliation also has appealed to scholars who argue that most white southerners never formed a strong allegiance to the Confederacy.

18. The most influential studies of Early's role in the Lost Cause movement are Gaines M. Foster's *Ghosts of the Confederacy: Defeat, the Lost Cause, and the Emergence of the New South* (New York: Oxford University Press, 1987) and Thomas L. Connelly's *The Marble Man: Robert E. Lee and His Image in American Society* (New York: Alfred A. Knopf, 1977), both of which portray Early as a mediocre Confederate general who dealt with his own failures and frustrations by putting Lee forward as a stainless hero after the war. Other titles that take a similar point of view are William Garrett Piston, *Lee's Tarnished Lieutenant: James Longstreet and His Place in Southern History* (Athens: University of Georgia Press, 1987), and Thomas L. Connelly and Barbara L. Bellows, *God and General Longstreet: The Lost Cause and the Southern Mind* (Baton Rouge: Louisiana State University Press, 1982). For an interpretation emphasizing Early's long-term success in molding the Confederate image, see Gary W. Gallagher, *Jubal A. Early, the Lost Cause, and Civil War History: A Persistent Legacy* (Milwaukee: Marquette University Press, 1995).

19. R. E. Lee to Jubal A. Early, November 22, 1865, March 15, 1866, George H. and Katherine Davis Collection, Howard-Tilton Memorial Library, Tulane University, New Orleans; Jubal A. Early to R. E. Lee, November 20, 1868, John Warwick Daniel Papers, Alderman Library, University of Virginia, Charlottesville.

20. Jubal A. Early, *The Campaigns of Gen. Robert E. Lee. An Address by Lt. Gen. Jubal*

A. Early, before Washington and Lee University, January 19th, 1872 (Baltimore: John Murphy & Co., 1872), pp. 45, 50–54.

21. Foster's *Ghosts of the Confederacy* offers the most detailed examination of the ways in which former Confederates remembered and celebrated the war. Not surprisingly, Foster argues that Lost Cause ideology had its greatest impact during the lives of those who experienced the conflict: "It helped explain to late nineteenth-century southerners how and why they lost the war that marked the end of the Old South. It helped them cope with the cultural implications of defeat. It served to ease their adjustment to the New South and to provide social unity during the crucial period of transition. But once it had done these things, the Lost Cause declined in utility and therefore in importance." By the early twentieth century, "the Confederate tradition played a limited role in modern southern culture" (p. 8). Charles Reagan Wilson's *Baptized in Blood: The Religion of the Lost Cause, 1865–1920* (Athens: University of Georgia Press, 1980) also contains useful insights about the process by which former Confederates came to terms with defeat. For a pictorial roster of hundreds of monuments, see Ralph W. Widener, Jr, *Confederate Monuments: Enduring Symbols of the South and the War Between the States* (Washington, D.C.: Andromeda Associates, 1982). A perceptive analysis of Lost Cause popular art, together with dozens of excellent color and black-and-white reproductions of important prints, may be found in Mark E. Neely, Jr., Harold Holzer, and Gabor S. Boritt, *The Confederate Image: Prints of the Lost Cause* (Chapel Hill: University of North Carolina Press, 1987).

INDEX

....

....